SPECIES

Mikado Pheasant
(*Syrmaticus mikado*)

Cheer Pheasant
(*Catreus wallichi*)

White Eared-Pheasant
(*Crossoptilon crossoptilon*)

Imperial Pheasant
(*Lophura imperialis*)

Palawan Peacock-Pheasant
(*Polyplectron emphanum*)

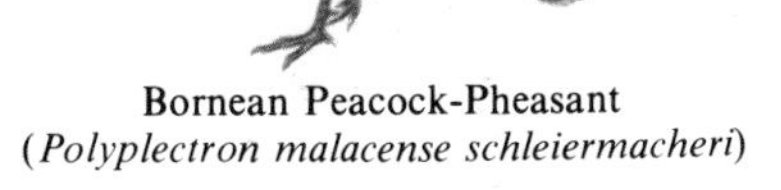

Bornean Peacock-Pheasant
(*Polyplectron malacense schleiermacheri*)

Cabot's Tragopan
(*Tragopan coboti*)

Blyth's Tragopan
(*Tragopan blythi*)

PHEASANTS

Their Breeding and Management

The Neelum Valley Azad Kashir – excellent Pheasant country.

PHEASANTS

Their Breeding and Management

K. C. R. Howman

Series Editor
Dennis Kelsey-Wood

The Bird Keeper's Library

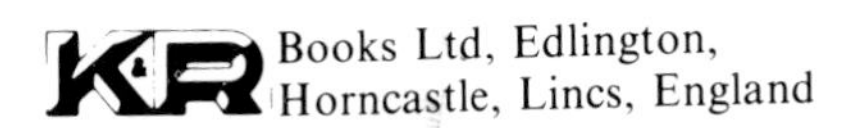
Books Ltd, Edlington,
Horncastle, Lincs, England

First published 1979
by K & R Books Ltd.,
Edlington, Lincolnshire

Cover Painting: Golden Pheasant by Esdaile Hudson

ISBN 0 903264 35 8

Typeset by Woolaston Parker Ltd, and printed in Great Britain by Litho Letterpress Service, both of Leicester and bound in Edinburgh by Hunter & Foulis Ltd.

CONTENTS

ACKNOWLEDGEMENTS

I would like to record my thanks to those many people who have helped and encouraged me in the hobby of keeping ornamental pheasants, in particular my colleagues in the World Pheasant Association with their President, Dr Jean Delacour, to whom we all owe so much. To their Secretary, Major Iain Grahame and Dr T. W. I. Lovel my special thanks for their help, assistance and advice in the writing of this book.

My thanks also to my secretary, Pat Skelton, for many long hours of patient typing from my pages of horribly-written manuscript – but particularly my thanks are due to my wife Jean who spent many hours after midnight reading, correcting, re-reading and advising – and who was always correct!

K. C. R. HOWMAN

Editor's Acknowledgements

Whilst endorsing my thanks to all those people mentioned by the author might I add also the following people without whom the finished book would have been the poorer. Esdaile Hudson, for his masterly paintings, Jean Howman for her superb photography, A. D. Forbes-Watson for his research on general authors and dates, Alan Webster for his line drawings and finally to John Gaten whose counsel is always worthwhile.

PREFACE

I was delighted to accept the invitation to write this book because I remember so well that when I first began to keep ornamental (as opposed to game) pheasants there was an almost total dearth of practical advice available at a reasonable price in a written form.

This book is not intended in any way to be a scientific book, nor is it expected or intended to become a standard reference on the subject. My own experience is that each year I learn something new either from the birds themselves or from fellow enthusiasts.

I have attempted to provide enough information to enable a beginner to start with confidence. My advice to any reader is not to take any of the information given as infallible, although it is I hope sound, but be prepared to experiment – within reason.

Finally, may I wish readers of this book as much pleasure and satisfaction from their hobby as I have had and continue to enjoy from the keeping of these fascinating birds.

K. C. R. Howman
Shepperton
1978

A pair of White Crested Kalij (*Lophura leucomelana hamiltoni*).

Chapter 1

INTRODUCTION

Pheasants belong to a family that includes some of the most beautiful birds in the world. Birds such as the Golden Pheasant, famous in Chinese art, have delighted and benefited man for centuries but sadly many of them are today under threat as a result of his activities.

There are forty-eight different species of pheasants, a fact which often surprises many people who think of a pheasant only as 'that delicious bird on the dining table'. All but one of the forty-eight species come from Asia, and can be split very simply between the high altitude species, which are totally hardy to snow and frost, living mainly in the Himalayas or the higher mountain areas of Japan and Formosa, and the low altitude species (mainly from Malaysia and the Phillipines) which do, in certain cases, need some heat and protection to enable them to survive without problems in winters with temperatures below freezing point.

Species range from the lovely Tragopans and Monal Pheasants living at altitudes of up to 14,000 feet (4,200m), to the Peacock-Pheasants, some of which live almost at sea level. Between these extremes we have the Junglefowl. Many people are not aware that the incredible variety of domestic poultry including such diverse species as Polish Bantams, Millefleurs, Brahmas, Battery hens and Fighting cocks are all derived from a pheasant – the Red Junglefowl – or that the Indian Blue Peafowl is in fact a pheasant. Pheasants belong to the order *Galliformes* which includes Grouse, Francolins and Partridge as well as less well known birds such as Curassows and Megapodes.

According to the last issue of the IUCN Red Data Book no less than one-third of the forty-eight pheasant species are already officially listed as in danger of dying out in their original habitat – a horrifying fact which immediately gives added value to the hobby of pheasant aviculture. It is perhaps the only branch of aviculture where, for a very modest sum, a pair of an endangered species can be bought and offspring successfully reared. Eight of the sixteen endangered species are quite freely available from pheasant aviculturists.

Later in this book we shall be examining some of the methods of keeping pheasants in captivity. Before doing this however, it may be of interest to look briefly at the reasons why so many of the pheasant species appear to be in danger of extinction.

Basically, most pheasants are forest dwellers and all but one species, the Congo Peafowl, come from Asia. Almost the whole of Asia has rapidly expanding human populations who require more and more land from which to derive a living. Fertilisers, modern farming equipment and expertise are necessary in order to produce more food at the lower and more suitable altitudes.

At present, the forests are being destroyed at an alarming rate in order to produce fuel and building materials on the one hand, and to make available more farming land on the other. The farming land at the forest altitudes is largely unsuitable for efficient farming, and after a few monsoon seasons the topsoil has been washed into the rivers in the valleys below and from there is carried to the plains where silting contributes greatly to the annual monsoon floods. With

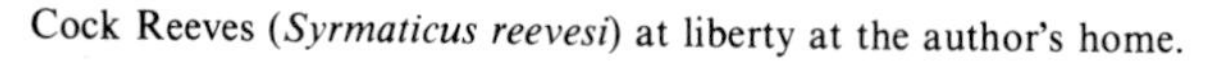
Cock Reeves (*Syrmaticus reevesi*) at liberty at the author's home.

Black-Breasted Kalij (*Lophura leucomelana moffitti*).

the forest destruction goes also the wildlife, including the pheasants.

Understanding is at last being reached that Asia cannot afford to continue to create desert where once there was forest. Some replanting is under way, but will probably never replace the wonderful natural mixed trees and shrub forests that were there before. Felling is still far outstripping replanting, but slowly it is hoped that the balance will be restored and those pheasant species that have been driven out in the process can be re-established from captive stocks using the knowledge and expertise built up by pheasant aviculturists.

To keep healthy genetically sound stock requires a sizeable 'gene pool' and care should be taken on the part of the breeder, as will be emphasised in a later chapter, to ensure that pairs are from as widely dispersed genetic lines as possible. It requires many people in many countries to take up the hobby, and it is hoped that the information in this book may encourage more to so do. In what other branch of aviculture is it possible to keep and propagate so many beautiful and endangered species and at the same time contribute to conservation?

A study of the record of pheasant aviculture shows that many more rare and endangered species have been bred and are alive in captivity today than have ever been taken from the wild.

A well designed row of aviaries using boarding to good effect.

An attractive open plan range of aviaries designed by Mr R. Sawyer. The absence of boarding between aviaries improves the aesthetic appearance but can lead to attempted fighting between cock birds.

Chapter 2

AVIARIES: PRACTICAL CONSIDERATIONS

Aviary accommodation

It is an unfortunate fact that the cost of building aviaries of a suitable shape and size can often be more than the cost of a good pair of pheasants. Cost, also, is too often a factor limiting the builder from affording the aviary design he would like. Having stated this one must say that a beautiful pair of pheasants will certainly not be enhanced if housed in structures of rusty wire and second-hand galvanised sheeting. In general then, pheasant aviculturists would agree that money spent in good design and long-life materials is well worth the extra investment.

Aviary size

There are several schools of thought on this question and my own preference is for aviaries for a pair of pheasants to be around 200 sq. ft. (18.6 sq. m). However, there are species such as the Tragopans and Koklass where an aviary size nearer 400 sq. ft. (37 sq. m) is more suitable, and others such as Peacock-Pheasants where 100 – 150 sq. ft. (9.3 – 14 sq. m) appears to be quite sufficient. On the Continent smaller sizes are often successfully used. In Chapter 7 there are notes on each species with recommended aviary size and type which readers may find useful. It will be seen from the points made later in this chapter that there are many factors to take into account when determining size, not least of which is the amount of space available.

Note: All conversions of measurements from British to Metric are approximates only and will suffice for the purpose of suggested sizes.

Aviary building materials

Choice of building materials must depend in many cases on aesthetic considerations, but basically one is dealing with different types of framework, netting and solid panelling for shelters.

Framework

Here choice really only lies between timber and metal. For the average handyman the former is more easily obtainable in varying sections and lengths and being more easily cut and fixed it is normally selected. Certainly my preference is for wood treated with a suitable preservative as being more sympathetic to the landscape, but having said this some excellent-looking aviaries have been constructed using tubular steel sections. The amateur, however, unless he is a metal-worker by trade, finds it easier and cheaper to make up his structures using timber, whether rustic or prepared.

One general comment on the structural framework of an aviary is that the pull on the main posts that can take place with snow loading on overhead netting should not be underestimated. For external framing posts 3″ × 3″ (7.6 × 7.6cm) section is a minimum, particularly for the corners.

Netting

Netting presents a choice of gauges and types. The first decision to make is whether to build sparrow-proof aviaries, or whether to be satisfied with containment of the birds. If the former, then ¾″ (2cm) mesh is the largest size possible, and ½″ (1.3cm) is preferable. The smaller gauges are more expensive, but the saving in feed and reduction of disease risk can be an overriding factor!

The only slight disadvantage of the smaller meshes is the aesthetic one of the wire being more obtrusive. This can, however, be reduced by application to the galvanised netting of a liquid bitumen. Syntha-prufe applied by roller can be recommended for this. It has the additional advantage of considerably increasing the life of the wire which is an important consideration. Wire netting of 18swg. is considered safe against most predators, and particularly in sparrow-proof mesh where, because of the small mesh size, it is impossible for a dog or fox to get hold of the wire with its teeth in order to tear at it. Where outside netting meets the ground it is wise to bring the netting down to the base of the supporting posts, out a foot (31cm) and then to dig it a foot (31cm) into the ground.

The alternative to wire netting is the increasingly popular black polythene netting which is now available in a variety of gauges and meshes. It appears to have very good resistance to ultra violet denegration and maintains its remarkable strength well. It can be recommended particularly for the roofing of pens where it has a great

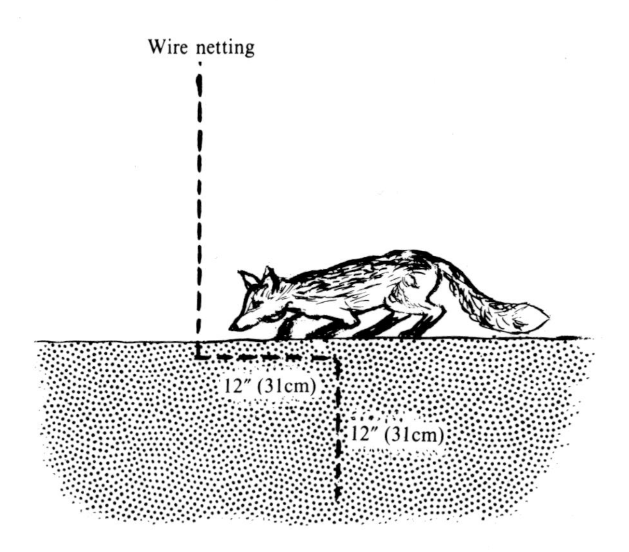

Diagram shows how digging-in of the netting the correct way prevents predators gaining entry into the aviary.

advantage in that it can be purchased in one piece to cover the aviary or aviaries concerned. Being more flexible than wire netting there is less risk of damage to a bird that happens to fly into the roof netting. It is risky for external side netting as rodents can, and do, gnaw through it.

Further materials will come in for comment as we look at a few aviary designs.

Aviary designs

Before starting aviary construction it is a considerable advantage to decide on the type of pheasant one is intending to keep. The main consideration is whether the aviary is to house a species that is totally hardy, needing good shelter but no heat, or one that requires some heat in order to survive the winter.

Hardy species

Let us start by assuming that we are going to construct an aviary for a hardy species, such as members of the genus *Syrmaticus*, or Long-tailed Pheasants, for example the Hume's or Reeves. The aviary size should be about 200 sq. ft. (18.6 sq. m). The next consideration is shape, which is often decided by available space. Assuming this is not the case, then we can make the shape suit the birds rather than the circumstances.

It is usual to have a shelter at the back of an aviary, or line of aviaries, to which the birds can retreat and my experience, and that of most aviculturists, is that a longish aviary with fairly narrow frontage is preferred by the birds to one with a long frontage and shallow depth. The reason is that in the former the birds can, if they wish, retreat to the back where they feel safe, whilst in an aviary with a depth, for example, of only 10 ft. (3m) and frontage of 20 ft. (6m), the pheasants can never get far away from something or someone they do not like.

If the objective is show, rather than breeding, then the pen of shallow depth may have an advantage although with some species even this is questionable. A bird that feels secure is more likely to come close than one that feels insecure and only wants to hide – it is also more likely to breed.

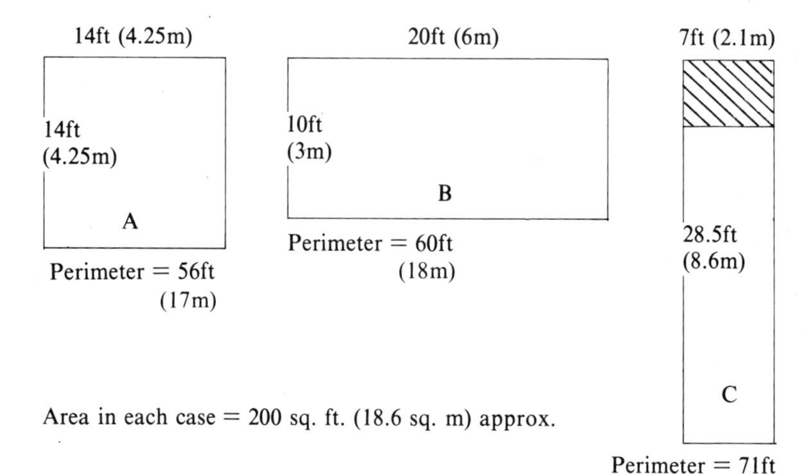

Vieillot's Crested Fireback (*Lophura ignita rufa*).

The square shape 'A' is the most economic with materials used in terms of perimeter, but is not ideal when it comes to including a shelter to provide a dry dusting area where birds can also escape from rain and wind if they wish. Ideally shelters should be of around 30 – 40 sq. ft. (2.8 – 3.7 sq. m), but it is difficult to have this with shape 'A' without leaving a lot of awkward right angles and a slightly untidy appearance.

The same comment applies to design 'B', though this is obviously good from the point of view that the birds are likely to be viewed easily. Design 'C' is the one generally favoured with the back area (shaded) forming the shelter. The construction of the shelter can be of larch-lap fence panelling, or close timber boarding roofed over with corrugated PVC sheeting. Design 'C' is also ideal for a line of aviaries, and it should be remembered that when adding new aviaries to an existing line it requires only three more sides and not the four needed for a separate new pen. The other advantage of this design is that it provides enough length of aviary to make the roofing-in of the front 6 ft. (1.8m) of the aviary a sensible proposition. The purpose of this is to provide a dry clean feeding area, away from the main collections of droppings which will be under the roosting perches in the shelter at the back. On a rainy day this means that the birds can eat their pellets in the dry – pellets become soggy within minutes and pheasants will not eat them in this condition. Sand is the ideal base under the roofed area.

Too often one has seen collections, on a wet day, with piles of soggy feed left untouched by the pheasants. This often starts to go mouldy or attract vermin, both with their likely attendant problems.

Boarding between aviaries

When constructed in a row, the question arises as to whether there should be boarding between aviaries. Birds tend to pace up and down along the dividing netting, and panelling prevents fighting between pheasants in adjacent pens. On the whole, most pheasant aviculturists favour boarding of 18″ – 24″ (46 – 61cm) in height, but I have tried omitting this in a new line of aviaries with no harmful results. From an aesthetic point of view, which is an important one, omitting divisional boarding does give a more attractive 'open plan' effect, but small-mesh netting is advisable for safety.

Major Iain Grahame, one of the leading aviculturists in England, changed from having boarding between pens to just netting with no serious problems. Another of his ideas is the design which provides a

Plan of aviary design with different sized aviaries but standardised shelters at the rear.

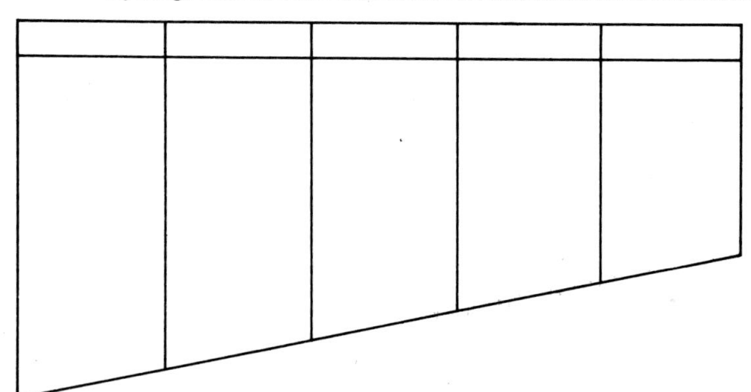

common straight line back shelter, for ease of building, with variation in the size of aviary. The idea is to house the birds that require least space in the small aviaries, and vice-versa.

Aviary floors

We have looked in part at one or two simple shapes and sizes as well as the simple caging materials, but so far without examining the floor or base of the aviary. This is probably the most important part and certainly is the area most open to discussion and debate. Deciding what the floor of the aviary is to be is fundamental to keeping pheasants in captivity, and should if possible be done at the building stage rather than changing later.

The first decision to make is whether to opt for a grass base or some alternative. Factors governing the decision are available space, drainage of the ground and again aesthetic consideration and type of inhabitant.

Grass

Koklass Pheasants, for example, require plenty of green food including grass, while Edwards' Pheasants by contrast seem to be uninterested in green food. This does mean, in the case of the former, that the grass is constantly being mown and a large aviary is required if the grass is to survive without protection. Most people would agree that well grassed aviaries look best. If muddy aviaries are anticipated then it is probably wise not to attempt to have grassed areas but to put down sand – preferably 'sharp' sand as the stone inclusion makes ideal grit and is not large enough to cause impacted gizzards. Some people do use pea gravel, but this can be dangerous, particularly for species like Tragopans which are inclined to show-off by picking it up, and then swallowing it by mistake.

Sand

If sand is to be used it is best to put it into the aviary before construction is started. A minimum depth of 6″ (15cm) and ideally 9″ – 12″ (23 – 30cm) is necessary. The labour of putting it in through narrow aviary doors afterwards is immense. Earth worms (one of the invertibrate hosts of the gape worm – *Syngamus trachea* – of which more later) are reluctant to work up through such a depth of dry material from which they can derive nothing. Sand always looks clean, can be raked over, and in the event of trouble can be very effectively treated with fumigants.

Wire mesh

Where grass has been selected and is found to be suffering from damage or a long wet winter, one effective solution is to lay down $1\frac{1}{2}'' \times 1\frac{1}{2}''$ (3.8 × 3.8cm) battens with a $\frac{1}{2}''$ (1.3cm) wire netting mesh or weldmesh covering. The grass will recover and grow up through it; the roots cannot be destroyed and soil-born diseases are reduced. During the spring and summer the grass will regrow and completely cover the battening. This method is particularly suited to vegetarian pheasants, such as the Koklass.

Aviary furniture

Perches are essential and should be under the shelter. They must not be too thin in diameter as the birds toes will curl right round them and remain exposed when the pheasant relaxes down on the perch. The thickness of a persons arm is ideal so that the feathers on the underside

Satyr Tragopan Cock (*Tragopan Satyra*). Note the mesh netting used to protect the grassed aviary floor.

A Cock Koklass Pheasant (*Pucrasia macrolopha*) in an aviary with mesh floors well covered by the grass growing through.

of the bird will be able to insulate the toes from frost. From an aesthetic point of view natural branches are preferable to sawn timber.

Decorative logs can improve the look of an aviary and also benefit the birds as they like to hop up and down on them to see what is going on round about. Rocks, such as Westmoreland, make an attractive addition or alternative.

Nest boxes are dealt with in a later chapter, but it is wise to plan your aviary layout with a view to providing good nesting cover which should be natural if possible.

Equipment, such as feeders and drinkers, is largely a matter of choice. Automatic watering systems usually work well, except during freezing conditions, though some systems are more difficult to keep

A Golden Pheasant (*Chrysolophus pictus*) seen in a very well planted aviary which shows off the bird to full effect.

clean than just a plain plastic dish. Feeding hoppers are normally unnecessary except when *ad lib* feeding is being provided and must be kept in dry conditions.

Aviary protection

Ornamental pheasants are valuable – some in terms of money and some in terms of rarity. They should be protected as far as possible from predators, both two legged and four legged. For the former the best protection is proximity to the home, but if this is not practical there are many alarm systems that can be fitted, some of which are quite inexpensive.

The four legged predators are the greatest risk, with foxes being the prime problem, closely followed by stoats, weasels, cats and grey squirrels. By far the most effective deterrent to foxes is an electric fence. Many makes are available, some operating on dry cell batteries, some on car batteries and others on mains electricity. Two wires are advisable, set about 1½ ft. (46cm) back from the outside aviary netting. The bottom wire should be about 4″ (10cm) above the ground, and the top wire about 8″ – 12″ (20 – 30cm) above the ground.

The smaller predators, such as the stoat and weasel, are likely to avoid an electric fence although if you have them in your area a good plan is to fix an electric fence wire into the perimeter posts to the aviary 4″ – 6″ (10 – 15cm) off the ground. The standard insulators will keep the wire 1″ – 2″ (2.5 – 5cm) clear which may solve the problem. The most certain protection however is ½″ (1.3cm) wire mesh netting.

Most aviaries have netted roofs and therefore raptores are not a problem unless perches are in the open and so close to the roof that the roosting bird's head is almost touching it. The solution is simple, move the perch under the shelter where it should be.

Non-hardy species

In the previous paragraphs we have covered the simple basic requirements for the hardy, principally Himalayan, species, together with a number of basic fundamental points on aviary design and construction. The requirements of the semi-tropical species, such as the Palawan Peacock-Pheasant, the Argus or the Bornean Crested Fire-back are similar in all respects except for the open-fronted shelter which is all that the hardy species require by way of cover and protection.

In the section covering pheasant species their individual requirements have been noted. Some only need their shelters to be kept just above freezing temperature while others, such as those mentioned above, will do much better given some heat. A temperature of 50° F is more than sufficient and can be obtained in a number of ways.

First of all, a simple boarded-in shed type structure is required. Ideally this should have windows at the back, unless it is part of a larger complex with a roofed-in corridor at the back, in which case there may be artificial lighting. Entry for the birds into the open-air part of the aviary should be through a trap door which can be opened and closed from the front of the aviary or the back by means of a string.

Heating system

Methods found to be effective include:

(i) Under floor heating – this is successful in the prime objective but does seem for some reason to encourage the irritating mite that causes scaly leg. This can be mitigated by creosoting all timber.

(ii) Tubular heating – this should be wired into a thermostat to prevent wastage of electricity.
(iii) Fan heaters – this method I have found very effective and surprisingly does not seem to upset the birds. A 1kw fan heater with built-in thermostat designed for horticultural purposes is used.

In America, at Mr Charles Sivelle's collection, a large oil fired industrial heater is used in a long shed with a central corridor and shelters on either side.

Artificial lighting

There are advantages in being able to lengthen the daylight hours – particularly with Peacock-Pheasants. It is worth considering at the construction stage putting in lighting which can be wired to a thermodim dimmer for the purposes of inducing early laying. See Chapter 6.

Special aviary design

Finally in this section a few ideas on aviary design of a more ambitious nature. The perfect pheasant aviary design from both a management and aesthetic viewpoint is the 'cart-wheel' design. This is illustrated with a line drawing. The principal features of this design are that only one external gate is necessary with all others being internal in the 'hub' of the cart-wheel. The hub contains a roofed-over feeding area so that all feeding can be done from the centre, under cover.

The basic design is almost as suitable for pheasants requiring heat as for those that do not – indeed, a mixture of the two is possible though extra access gates between or within pens would be necessary where the front of the shelters, shaded in the diagram, are boarded up to retain heat.

Only one aspect of the design is wasteful, which is the roof netting, and here the purchasing of black polythene netting in a square large enough to cover the entire area is recommended. A friend of mine who tried to do it in pieces for economy and had numerous joints regretted his decision after hours of tedious work.

Another good aviary design is one based on an old stable block, pighouse or similar building of long rectangular shape. By using the

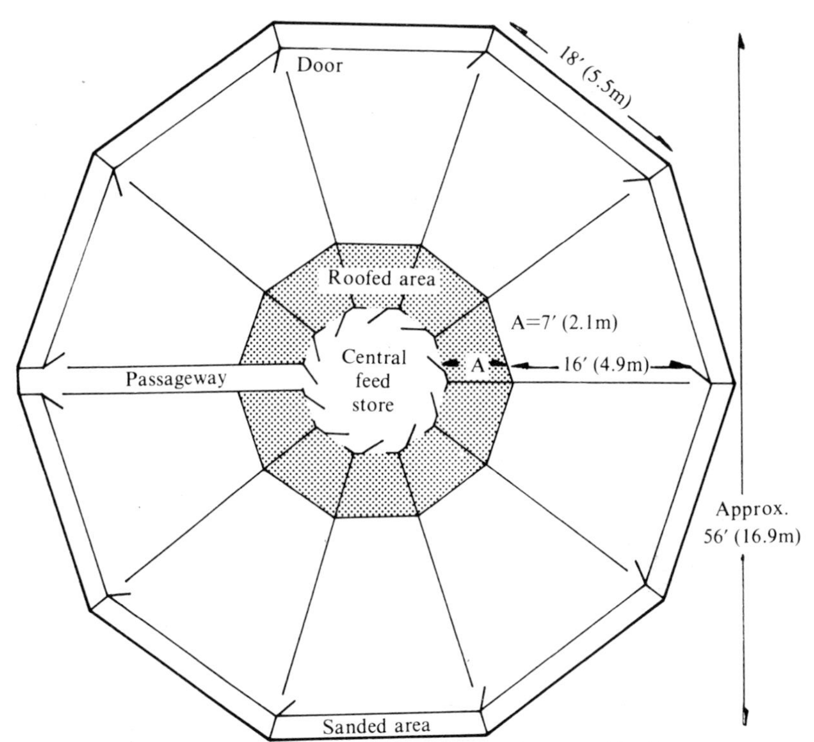

Circular aviary design. Note single access gate and central store and feeding room.

An aviary based upon an old stable block or pighouse.

7	Central corridor		1
8			2
9			3
10			4
11			5
12			6

Notes:

1. Popholes so that birds can be transferred from one aviary to an adjacent one without handling are an advantage;
2. Only a pophole which can be opened and shut by means of a string is necessary between the open part of the aviary and the enclosed shelters in 7 – 12;
3. Peacock-Pheasants only need fairly small 'open air' aviaries compared to other species.

main building for the internal shelters with a corridor down the centre, management of the pens is made easy – an automatic watering system can also be effectively installed as freezing-up in winter would be unlikely. Outside runs are fitted as shown in the drawing.

If an existing building is not available then the design shown is again ideal from a management point of view. The internal lining to the corridor can be either wire, solid timber or even glass, providing it is covered by a flexible netting, or a combination of the two with aviaries 1 to 6 having only wire lining, and aviaries 7 to 12 having fully enclosed shelters for semi-tropical species.

Many variations of shape, size and materials are, of course, possible. The main points to remember are the requirements of the birds and your own ease of administration.

Aviary planting

It would seem a pity to spend considerable time and money on building suitable aviaries and not to give thought to their planting with shrubs. Not only does a well landscaped aviary look nice, it also results in more settled and contented birds.

Pheasants can however be most destructive where plants are concerned and can quickly devastate a newly planted aviary. For this reason it is essential to protect particularly roots and stems. Brown or green plastic vinyl netting is ideal and is not obtrusive.

Some species are more destructive than others. Cheer, Monal and all the Eared-Pheasants are diggers and will damage root systems. Golden Pheasants will be more likely to destroy the leaves.

In planting an aviary a balance should be provided between the larger shrubs which provide shade and shelter and possible roosting sites, and the lower growing shrubs for hiding or natural nesting cover.

Smaller pheasants, such as the Peacock-Pheasants do not destroy plants and therefore less tough and perhaps more decorative shrubs including heaths and heathers may be grown.

Plants which have been found to grow well in pheasant aviaries have been listed in their different categories below.

Climbers

Plants which will climb and cover bare supporting posts or screen pens from each other include:

Climbing roses, *Lonicera* (honeysuckle), Jasmine – both white and winter yellow, Vines and Virginia creepers, variegated Ivies, Clematis, Passion flower, canary creeper (an annual) Polygonum or Russian vine and Pyracantha. Some of these will have to be tied to their supporting posts.

Grasses and Bamboos

Some of these will grow very quickly and make good bushy cover at ground level. Pampas grasses *Cortaderia* 5 – 8 ft. (1.5 – 2.4m) and Bamboos *Arundinaria* 6 – 9 ft. (1.8 – 2.7m) are good examples although the latter like time to establish. Variegated grasses such as *Miscanthus* will reach 6 – 7 ft. (1.8 – 2.1m), wood rushes *Luzula* and Golden grass *Milium* 1 – 2 ft. (30 – 61cm). The higher growing varieties can be cut down as necessary.

Quick growing shelter

If the idea is to have a fast growing evergreen hedge either for screening or for shelter, then the ideal plant is *Cupressocyparis leylandii*. This, when established, will put on 3 – 4 ft. (91 – 122cm) per year, and can easily be 'stopped' to form a thick hedge. Almost as fast growing and becoming increasingly popular is *Thuya lobbii excelsa*.

Evergreen shrubs

Most of these are hardy and tough and fairly resistant to the ravages of most pheasant species:

Box, Laurel, Bay laurel, *Lonicera nitida* both the dark green and the gold varieties. *Mahonias*, Privet common and golden. *Berberis* particularly *Berberis stenophylla* and *Berberis darwinii Viburnum tinus*. Lavenders, *Elaeagnus* species.

Ground cover plants

I have found many of the *Hebes* or Veronicas very satisfactory as birds can easily hide beneath them and they are colourful in foliage and flower. Choose varieties that grow to about two feet. *Hypericum calycinum* or the Rose of Sharon grows in any soil and well in shade. It is evergreen in most parts of the country. *Cotoneaster horizontalis* and *Cotoneaster damerii* provide excellent firm ground cover. Conifers for ground cover are mainly *Juniperus* but these are slow growing.

Shrubs

Those which will be found particularly good include many of the *Cotoneasters* particularly *C.franchetii*, *C.frigidus* and *C.salicifolius*, and varieties of the evergreen *Ceanothus*. These can be bought to flower from late spring through to the autumn and with their glossy holly-like small leaves are most attractive. Rhododendrons and evergreen Azaleas do well in certain soil conditions as also do shrub Roses. *Buddleias*, particularly *B.globosa* which is evergreen and *Kerria japonica* (Jews mallow), are fast growing. Buddleias are not for the smaller aviaries.

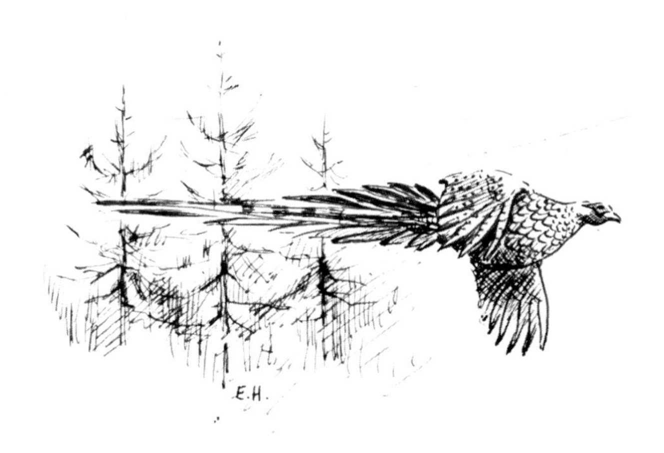

Chapter 3

GENERAL MANAGEMENT AND HUSBANDRY

The most important aspect of good pheasant aviculture, as with most forms of livestock management, is attention to care and detail. Anyone can rush out of the house after breakfast, throw a couple of handfuls of feed at the birds, and race for the factory. For long periods this may suffice, but certainly will not when a problem arises.

Just as a shepherd knows his flock and their individual habits, so should the pheasant keeper know his birds. Each one will have a different characteristic. Sometimes it is a shy bird that only comes forward to feed when you have passed on to the next aviary – or a greedy Cheer Pheasant that jumps up and attempts to take the feed from your hand – or the quiet little Kalij which stands patiently under the same bush each morning waiting to be fed. A change from any one of these characteristics can mean trouble – it certainly should be the signal to look out for. During the winter months it is likely to be trouble of some sort – in the spring it could be that the bird, if a hen, is about to lay.

Just as the birds have their routines, so should the pheasant aviculturist have his. Always try to feed at the same time, and start with the same pen and feed in the same order. This way the pheasants, which it should be remembered are basically shy, wary game birds, will become used to the routine and adapt themselves to it.

Ideally the same person should feed each day so that any changes of behaviour are noticed. This particularly applies to Zoos and Bird Gardens where there are perhaps several people in charge of the birds.

Common ailments

It is not intended in this book to provide a veterinary guide to pheasant diseases. Every conceivable and inconceivable disease has been well and truly covered by the Poultry Industry and the pheasant aviculturist who wishes to frighten himself should obtain the *Salsbury Manual of Poultry Diseases* or the *Poultry Servicemans*

Manual from Merck Sharp & Dohme. A short practical booklet called *Some Diseases of Gamebirds and Waterfowl* published by the Game Conservancy can be recommended.

However, having started this chapter by emphasising the need to be on the lookout for trouble, a few brief notes on what sort of problems are most likely to occur and how they can be diagnosed may be helpful.

The phrase 'how you can diagnose it' has been used advisedly because it is the experience of most aviculturists that they often have to carry out their own diagnosis – partly because few veterinarians have much practical knowledge (as opposed to theoretical) of how the birds look and react when sick, and partly because it is really seldom sensible to catch the bird and carry it down to their surgery – indeed, more harm than good is likely to result. The alternative is an expensive visit by the veterinary surgeon.

Daily observation of the birds is the greatest help in providing clues for a correct diagnosis. Before describing a few of the common ailments it is worth stressing that if a bird dies and it is not known for certain what the cause was, a post-mortem should be conducted. Observation of the symptoms leading up to death and then finding out the cause is the quickest way to learn how to diagnose that particular disease in the future.

One other useful form of fairly positive diagnosis that a laboratory can provide is by the collection of the faecal droppings from a sick bird. These should be sent for analysis. This, usually, can positively identify heavy infestations of worms, Blackhead and Coccidiosis, and as these are three of the main pheasant problems, let us now deal with them in that order.

Gapeworm and roundworms

Gapeworm is the perfect problem to start with as self diagnosis is comparatively simple. *Syngamus trachea* as its scientific name implies is a nasty little creature which lodges in the throat or trachea of the pheasant. This causes irritation to the bird resulting in a pheasant form of 'coughing' which is a 'snicking' sound. An affected bird will open its beak wide and shake its head in an effort to dislodge the parasite.

Treatment is normally relatively simple using one of the proprietary wormers available based on the drugs Tetramisole hydrochloride, Mebendazole or Thiabendazole. The first two of these drugs are also fairly effective with roundworms. Roundworms can be in many forms, thread, hair and caecal worms, but do not usually cause serious problems to adult birds particularly for the first few years in the life of a new aviary.

Good practice is to start by treating against worms on a prophylactic basis twice a year, once in February before the start of the breeding season, and again around July or August after the breeding season at the start of the moult. If problems arise in between it might be advisable to increase this to four times a year either for all birds, or for the principal sufferers. There is a theory that a reasonable worm burden does no harm and builds up resistance to the worms and their effects.

Other than on a prophylactic basis or for specific treatment of an obviously affected bird it is a wise precaution to use a wormer the moment a bird is sick for any reason other than obvious physical damage. The reasons are twofold – firstly worms may be the problem anyway, and secondly, even if they are not, the worm burden in a sick bird can build up rapidly so that it is best to be rid of them.

Blackhead

A common disease in turkeys known as Blackhead can be a serious killer with pheasants. It is caused by the protozoa *Histomonas meleagridis* which is carried by the caecal worm *Heterakis gallinae*. It is a disease particularly common to peafowl, and in aviaries that have never had the problem it is likely that it will arise only through new stock. The treatment is very simple, using a drug called Emtryl premix in the food, or Emtryl soluble in the water. It is advisable to treat all new stock as if they have the disease on arrival as a precaution.

Because of its regular appearance in turkey flocks most turkey pellets contain Emtryl at a suppressive level – sufficient to prevent a sudden major outbreak.

Symptoms of blackhead are birds which become rapidly more miserable and have loose greenish or yellowish droppings. These should not, however, be confused with normal healthy dark brown rather loose droppings. These are the caecal droppings which are voided in a ratio of about 1:7 to droppings from the small intestine.

Coccidiosis

This is probably the most feared of all the diseases that strike both poultry and pheasants because it can cause havoc, particularly amongst young birds. It is a disease more usual in intensive rearing and particularly outdoor rearing where there are often damp conditions. It can be treated by using a sulpha drug such as Sulphadimidine or Sulphaquinoxaline. Feed can be obtained containing a controlling drug known as a Coccidiostat. This is to be recommended in chick crumbs, but not in maintenance or breeder rations as this is principally a disease of chicks and poults.

Under this section it is probably appropriate to mention that as Coccidiosis is a vicious form of enteritis so the latter problem should be watched out for. The symptoms again are a miserable, mopey looking bird usually producing a large number of whitish droppings. Treatment can be with a sulphur based drug, but it is probably better to use a wide spectrum antibiotic, such as Penbritin, as this would also cure several other problems should your initial diagnosis prove wrong.

Fowl pest or Newcastle disease

This is a viral disease – where treatment is not possible after an outbreak. Pheasants are on the whole very much more resistant than poultry, but do suffer from fowl pest. Prevention is very simple using either what is known as dead (inactivated vaccines) or live vaccines. The former can only be administered using a syringe as it is an injection usually put into the leg or breast muscle of the bird. Much simpler is the live vaccine Hitchner B1 which requires a drop into the eye of a bird at one day old and is quick and easy for young chicks. It can be administered in their drinking water but the other live vaccine La Sota should not be used before three weeks of age. For adult stock treatment twice each year should be sufficient before and after but not during the breeding season as it can upset laying birds.

Sinusitis

One other common disease in pheasants, particularly young ones, is sinusitis. It particularly affects the digging species such as the Brown Eared-Pheasant, Monal and Cheer. The symptoms are fairly easily spotted and are two-fold. One is a wet discharge from the nostrils, and the other is a foaming of minute bubbles looking exactly like 'Cuckoo spit' in the corner of the eye.

Treatment is simple with a drug called Tylan. Give the drug in the water in the prescribed way, and also if the foaming at the eye is bad, catch the bird and gently wash out its eye and clean the nostrils with cotton wool saturated with a solution of the same liquid. The latter is not a part of the generally prescribed treatment, but it does appear to hasten a cure.

General

Many times when a bird is cured it is not known exactly how this cure has been achieved. Providing that the vet agrees then every pheasant aviculturist with more than just a couple of pens should keep a small drugs cupboard stocked with the following:

A wormer, such as Mebenvet;
Emtryl against Blackhead;
Vesadin against Coccidiosis;
Terramycin or Penbritin – broad spectrum antibiotics;
Tylan for Sinusitis.

Administering medications

The golden rule is to avoid handling the birds if possible, therefore most medications are made to be suitable for mixing either into water or food. With the former it is necessary to remove all other sources of water and if there is time it is wise to deprive the bird of water for twelve to twenty-four hours beforehand.

For medications suitable for mixing into feed the problem is to try to make sure that the powder, which it is almost certain to be, is actually ingested by the bird. The principle to follow is the same as for treating young children. Try to make the food as attractive as possible and try to choose food to which the powder will adhere, or into which it can be mixed. There are many alternatives, but sultanas are one useful medium on their own particularly if the birds are used to them. A mixture of minced hard-boiled egg with added tidbits of peanuts, sultanas, etc., is usually easily accepted unless the bird is very sick.

For very sick birds that have 'gone off' their food, handling the bird and forced administration of the drug may be necessary. If it can be intramuscularly injected then this is the best method causing least stress. If it has to be given orally then the base part, as opposed to the needle part, of a disposable syringe is the ideal piece of equipment for any drug that is water soluble. For small volumes of liquid slow administration into the opened beak is all that is necessary allowing time for the bird to swallow after each few drops. For larger amounts a piece of valve tubing can be attached to the syringe and inserted gently down the throat in order to avoid liquid entering the lungs. The help of the local veterinary officer is strongly recommended particularly for the inexperienced pheasant keeper.

Ectoparasites

These are parasites living on the exterior surfaces of the birds.

The first of these is the mite which causes scaly leg. It burrows under the leg scales forming crusty deposits or lumps and making the legs look very unsightly. The mite appears to thrive on dry warmth and certainly the semi-tropical pheasant species, such as Argus, Bornean Crested Fireback and Palawan Peacock-Pheasants which have heated shelters seem to suffer particularly from it. It is very often started off by communication from a bantam foster mother to the chick, as indeed are two other pests, the feather louse and feather mite. These are very common on poultry and on a healthy bird do not usually get out of hand since they are always being removed by preening. On a sick bird they multiply rapidly and can be very much a contributory cause of death. Treatment for scaly leg, feather lice and mites necessitates catching the bird.

In the case of scaly leg, liquid paraffin is the base generally used and does indeed cure the problem on its own. The best known proprietary treatment is Gammexene, and many people mix the two together.

Coopers louse powder can be mixed into liquid paraffin and this also works well. An old toothbrush is an ideal applicator and should be used to brush the liquid well in. The treatment should be repeated after seven days.

Coopers louse powder is also the treatment against feather mites and lice. It should be liberally applied, particularly around the vent, the neck and under the wings.

Bantam flock

Care of a bantam flock is included under this section since it is my opinion that good management and husbandry of the 'few old bantams we keep around the place' is just as important as for the pheasants themselves. They are, in the first place, more likely to contact fowl pest, so do make sure that they have been vaccinated.

They should as a matter of routine be treated for scaly leg and lice twice each year. These birds will, for many, be the key to success or failure in hatching and rearing pheasant chicks during the breeding season. Chapter 6 deals in more detail with the handling of broody hens, but it is worth mentioning here that if the intention is to have good broody foster mothers, as much care should be taken in selecting from good broody stock and in breeding only from best birds for replacements, as would be taken in selecting pheasant stock.

Temmink's Tragopan (*Tragopan temmincki*) photographed at Jersey Zoo.

Chapter 4

FEEDING

The Western world is fortunate in having a very sophisticated poultry industry and careful research has resulted in balanced feeds of known protein, fibre and oil content which can be relied upon. Pheasant breeders over the past decade or more have found that in particular the feeds produced for turkeys provide almost all the basic requirements for most pheasant species.

Aviculturists in most of the Asian countries have a more difficult problem – the same problem indeed that the brilliantly successful aviculturists of the 1890s had; that of having to make up balanced rations from a number of available ingredients. It is interesting to look back and review the way in which they tackled the problem.

Old fashioned methods

First of all, wheat was known to be a good staple diet on which pheasants could survive with little else. Sunflower seeds which contain oil were fed to aid the moult after the breeding season. Soya bean and Sunflower seeds are also high in vegetable protein, and other seeds, such as Linseed and Goa also provided essential oils and it was soon discovered that pheasants have a great love for peanuts.

Vitamins used to be provided, not as we have them in pelleted poultry feeds, but by added cod liver oil for the fat soluble vitamins plus extra animal protein. One old gamekeeper recalled that on his estate, during the partridge and pheasant rearing season, a horse, cart and driver would be employed full time digging up ants' nests, and it was usual for gamekeepers to shoot rabbits and mince their paunches to provide the animal protein needed. Fresh minced meat is an alternative to the fish, meat or bonemeal included in pelleted feeds.

Modern poultry rations

Modern pelleted feeds can be broken down into three types. Breeder pellets, rearing or maintenance pellets and chick crumbs. Of the proprietary brands there are usually two types available, generally known as poultry or turkey pellets. The former usually have a protein content of 18 – 20 per cent for breeder pellets, 16 – 18 per cent for rearer pellets and 18 – 20 per cent for chick crumbs. On the whole pheasant breeders prefer turkey rations with a protein content about 5 per cent higher, though there is a danger, particularly with certain species, of killing through over-kindness. Certainly there are too many post-mortem cases where death appears to have been due in part to feeding a diet too rich in protein. The basic feeding system used in my aviaries is as follows.

Seasonal feeding

From mid-February 23 per cent protein breeder pellets (3.2mm) is fed in the morning, about 1½ oz. (43gms) per bird, and wheat in the afternoon, about ½ oz. (14gms) per bird. Wheat is high in energy but low in protein and tends to make birds fat. The afternoon feed is slowly replaced by breeder pellets until by the end of March most of the birds are on pellets only. This should continue until the end of

Sonnerat's Junglefowl Cock (*Gallus sonnerati*).

Blue Eared-Pheasant (*Crossoptilon auritum*).

May when wheat is re-introduced as the afternoon feed. By this time the first chicks are being hatched and are fed on 28 per cent protein chick crumbs to start with, graduating on to 23 per cent minipellets (2mm). Towards the end of August, when all chicks are at least six weeks old the change is made to 18 per cent protein maintenance pellets (3.2mm). In the case of young birds these are provided exclusively, whilst the adult birds still have wheat in the afternoon. Gradually wheat is mixed in for the young stock as well from eight weeks onwards, until a 50:50 mixture is reached.

Feeding methods and additional feeding

While aviculturists tend to be individualistic with the nutrition for their birds there are basically two main systems – hand feeding or *ad lib* hopper feeding. The former is the only satisfactory method if the aviaries are not of sparrow proof netting, and even if they are, hand feeding is preferable as it virtually guarantees that each bird is seen every day under conditions where its behaviour is likely to be the same. The value of this was emphasised in the previous chapter. Many breeders, however, particularly the Americans, many of whom are highly successful, believe in *ad lib* feeding of pellets but at a regular time each day, small quantities of popular tidbits such as peanuts and sultanas are fed in addition. It must be remembered that peanuts are fattening and ought to be used sparingly. This is the system that I have adopted for semi-tropical species.

Silver Pheasant (*Lophura leucomelana*) in a sanded aviary.

Special feeding and growing of feed

Some species do appear to have special requirements so a few comments on this may be helpful. Most pheasant species enjoy green food and it is undoubtedly good for them. In addition to fresh grass clippings, lettuce is a good stand-by and is appreciated by almost all species although a much cheaper and even preferable food is Chickweed. This can be fed in large quantities to all the vegetarian species such as the Tragopans and Koklass Pheasants. Swedes, sugar beet, carrot, and fruit such as apple, orange, banana and grapes are popular. A visit to the local greengrocer on a Saturday evening can be rewarding. If there is an orchard where windfall apples can be collected during the summer the birds will quickly take to them. Beware of suddenly introducing too much of one tidbit.

A most valuable form of additional feed that can be grown for birds is

Alfalfa also known as Lucerne. This crop starts from a seed which looks like 'cress' and grows just as rapidly. In warm sunny weather it will reach a couple of inches in height after four to five days and is at this stage ideal for feeding to young chicks. It has a protein content of well over 20 per cent which is unusual for an easily grown vegetable crop. If left to grow it attains a height of about 12″ (30cm) and can be cropped by cutting two or three times in a year. Some American and Canadian breeders also use it as bedding for young chicks in place of more conventional materials.

Compared to growing lettuce with its protein content of just over 1 per cent, Alfalfa is wonderful value but the former is nevertheless useful in providing minerals and vitamin A. To grow extra for the birds is to be encouraged. There is just one word of warning that should be made in respect of Alfalfa seed. It is a farming crop for cattle fodder and the seed is often 'dressed' with chemicals to discourage small birds as well as fungal growth. It is wise to ensure that the seed bought has not been so treated.

Live insect food

In the same way that growing of special vegetable crops can be beneficial in the feeding of pheasants, so too can the propagation of live insects. There are three insects worth considering although one of them, maggots, can have its disease risks and is probably best left to specialist supply companies.

The other two are locusts and mealworms. The former are more difficult to obtain initially and certainly more difficult to catch and feed to the birds once propagation has succeeded. Both require warmth and a suitable container. An empty small aquarium is ideal with the heat source being provided by a 60-watt lamp bulb.

Mealworms are both the cleanest and most practical insect to breed as all that is required is a few inches of bran in the bottom of the aquarium. Place in the bran a few thick slices of potato or apple and put the initial stock of mealworms into the aquarium, covering the bran with several layers of newspaper or sacking. The mealworms like getting between the layers where they can be easily collected. The life cycle of mealworms is fairly slow hence the reason they are expensive to buy. The mealworms themselves when mature become chrysalises and hatch fairly quickly into black beetles which mate and the female then lays eggs. These hatch initially into minute mealworms taking about four to six weeks to reach the stage where they are large enough to feed to the birds. However, though the reproductive cycle is fairly slow it is trouble free and they are at all times clean non-smelly little insects. There is nothing better for starting young chicks on, particularly the insectivorous Peacock-Pheasants.

Wild insects

Another source of animal protein has been utilised by the Americans by the use of special electric attractors and catchers of night flying insects. Working on the principle of light attraction they have a circular fluorescent bulb with a fan in the centre which knocks any insect touching it down into a plastic bag. In the morning there is a bag full of various insects. They certainly provide ideal extra feeding for young chicks. The units manufactured by F.E.I. Industries are advertised in American avicultural journals.

Grit

It would be wrong to end the chapter on the feeding of pheasants without mention of the process that assists the digestive mechanism. It is the action of grit in the bird's gizzard on the food which it eats that grinds it into a digestible paste. Grit is more important if grass forms part of the bird's diet. There are two principle forms of grit and each has a completely different purpose. The grit assisting digestion is granite or flint which are hard stones broken into small pieces and graded for size. There are sizes for chicks or small birds, and for larger birds. One normally supplies chick grit to young chicks over a couple of weeks old, and poultry grit to all the older birds. The latter, however, will not need much extra grit if they have sharp sand, either in their shelters or as a base to their feeding area from which they are able to pick plenty of suitable small stones. The other form of grit is Oyster shell or limestone which is soluble. This is intended for laying birds and should only be provided during the breeding season to replace the calcium that goes into making the egg shells. Whilst calcium is an essential mineral there is quite enough in pelleted feeds for normal requirements and excessive amounts do more harm than good, especially if the dietary content of Vitamin D is high. Oyster shell grit therefore is for the breeding season only.

Chapter 5

CHOICE OF SPECIES AND STOCK SELECTION

Species for beginners

The choice with which to start a collection is always a difficult decision. The Golden Pheasant, one of the most common species in captivity as well as probably the most colourful, is usually the most popular choice followed closely by the Silver or the Lady Amherst. They are not necessarily the best selection and all three species require two years to mature.

Pheasants which do not attain adult plumage in their first year normally take two or more years to become sexually mature although occasionally birds do mature in their first year due to the artificial conditions of captive breeding with high protein feeds. It is a good idea therefore to start either with a mature pair of any of the species mentioned above, or to buy a young pair of another inexpensive and easily managed variety such as the Reeves or Cheer. Compared to the aviary costs, or to the birds in other forms of aviculture, the initial

Hume's Bar-tailed Pheasant (*Syrmaticus h. humiae*).

cost of stock of the more abundant species is relatively low. Several species can be obtained at modest prices including Golden, Silver and Reeves Pheasants. Several of the endangered species such as Cheer, Elliot's, Hume's, Swinhoe's and Mikado Pheasants will cost you a higher price but still represent excellent value by today's standards. Management and breeding of endangered species provides much of the pleasure and satisfaction obtained from this hobby. Cheer, Elliot's, Hume's and Mikado Pheasants all mature in their first year, are all hardy, and are as easy to keep as a Golden or a Silver Pheasant.

It is prudent to confine oneself for the first year or two to the cheaper pheasants, and certainly it is wise to select the hardy high altitude species and leave the more delicate birds, such as the various Peacock-Pheasants until experience and confidence has been gained.

The purchase of stock

Perhaps the greatest weakness in pheasant aviculture is inbred stock. This derives from the tendency for each breeder to keep only one pair of several species rather than several pairs of one species. As a result each breeder can only offer brother and sister pairs for sale, and most purchasers usually buy their pairs, for convenience, from one supplier. If brother and sister pairs are used for too many generations, problems, such as lack of fertility and reluctance to mate result.

When making the initial purchase ensure that the pair is unrelated if possible. This can be done in three ways:

(a) Buying the cock and hen birds from different sources. This sounds considerably easier than is often the case as people tend to sell pairs, and with almost all species the hen birds are in shorter supply than cock birds. It should be ensured that the hen bird is purchased first as it is most irritating to purchase a cock bird and then be unable to locate a hen.

(b) Buy from a reputable dealer after giving clear instructions that an unrelated pair is required. The larger dealers handle such large numbers of pheasants that making up unrelated pairs, or at least pairs that are not closely related to each other, is usually a simple matter. The better dealers perform a most valuable service to pheasant aviculture.

(c) This method is the most reliable – buy two pairs of the same species from different sources, then select the cock and hen from the two pairs. The surplus pair can then be sold as an unrelated pair!

Success begets success and it is the breeders who consistently have good results who are the best ones to buy from as it is likely that they have selected their stock carefully in the first place.

Finally, beware of 'adult' stock. Whilst certain adult birds come on the market because a mate has suddenly died from some natural cause, or a collection is being reduced, a high percentage are sold for a variety of not such good reasons. They may have killed their mate, or be so old as to be infertile or they may have proved infertile for a number of years. In general, therefore, young birds should be purchased.

Although game pheasants are sold as eggs, day old chicks, or 7 – 8 week old poults, this is seldom done with ornamental pheasants which are normally sold at the stage that they start to 'colour up', around 12 – 14 weeks of age. Eggs are seldom sold because of the difficulty in putting a fair price on eggs that may or may not be fertile, and may or may not hatch. The normal poult stage for game pheasants of 6 – 8 weeks is generally too young for most ornamental species to be moved safely as they are seldom fully hardened off.

By 12 – 14 weeks old, birds should be well feathered and in the case of all the hardier species fully acclimatised to outdoor weather conditions. Whilst poor looking birds do from time to time prove to be good breeders it is wise to attempt to begin with perfect birds. A common fault with artificially reared birds is twisted toes and on the whole birds with this fault are better avoided, particularly if they are cock birds. It has been suggested that this problem is caused by in-breeding. It is more likely to have been caused by imperfect incubator conditions, dietary deficiences in parent birds or chicks, or excessive infra-red brooder lamp heat.

Young birds too should be purchased fully feathered and not minus tail and back feathers due to feather pecking. Birds denuded of feathers cannot be expected to survive wet outdoor conditions in the way that a properly feathered bird can – so if you have the chance to see the birds before accepting delivery, avoid those which have been feather pecked.

Cock Sonnerat's Junglefowl (*Gallus sonnerati*) showing the full cape for which this species was in such demand for trout and salmon flies.

Chapter 6

THE BREEDING SEASON

The breeding season is the high point of every pheasant aviculturist's year and there is little to match the excitement for a beginner of the arrival of the first egg. To acquire this egg demands good preparation, starting many weeks before.

Preparation

It is useless to wait until the first egg arrives before deciding on the form of incubation to be used for its hatching. There are two principal alternatives, incubators or broody hens, and the decision is a difficult one. A well behaved broody hen will always give a better hatching result than an incubator – however, not all hens that go broody are well behaved throughout the incubation period and they require far more time and management. They also require considerably more space. Let us examine these two alternatives in detail.

Incubators

Most breeders of ornamental pheasants only keep smallish numbers of birds and therefore only require a small sized incubator. Until a few years ago all the small ones available on the market were of the type known as 'Still Air'. This is a slight misnomer since they do have ventilation and slow air movement caused by convection. 'Still Air' machines basically have little air movement and in general have been found to give excellent hatching results when used for the final three days of incubation but indifferent results when used for the whole incubation period.

A few years ago the first of the small moving air incubators came on the market. These were of American manufacture and incorporated an automatic egg turning device. They are in effect miniature versions of the large commercial incubators manufactured for the poultry and game farming industries and incorporate a small fan in the dome of the incubator. In general all the incubators of around 100 egg capacity have excellent temperature control. Humidity control is inclined to be much less exact. The experience with the large commercial incubators is that eggs should be transferred from the moving air incubator into 'still air' hatchers about three days prior to hatching.

Although most moving air machines are claimed to be able to hatch from start to finish much better results are invariably obtained when still air hatchers are used in conjunction with them. My own experience with the small Marsh Roll-X moving air incubator is similar and a combination of the two types of machine is now used with good results.

Incubator housing

Incubator manufacturers will usually provide advice on location of their machines. Much of the success of small incubators lies in their being located in a suitable room. The room should be of as even a temperature as possible and should not heat up dramatically in the summer months. Garden sheds of asbestos or timber construction are not usually very good whereas wine cellars are ideal.

Broody hens

It has been said with a good deal of truth that there should be as much care in the selection and breeding of a good bantam flock (for

A Marsh Roll-X automatic incubator in use.

broodiness) as in the choice of the pheasant stock. One can selectively breed for 'broodiness' in the same way as one can for particular colour strains. Some breeders use only Silky bantams, but my preference is for Silky bantams crossed with other bantam species. One well-known breeder puts leg bands of different colours on his hens depending on the number of successful broods that they have hatched. Only those that have hatched three or more clutches successfully are penned separately at the end of the season with a cock bird and used for breeding replacements and additional stock for the following year.

Health of bantam flock

Chickens are capable of carrying some diseases which if passed to young pheasant chicks will result in their death. For this reason it is wise to be particularly careful to keep a bantam flock under good healthy conditions and to treat the birds prior to the breeding season against a number of possible diseases and parasites.

February is the month to make preparations and to ensure that the flock is in the best possible health for the following months. Birds should be treated against fowl pest and also thoroughly wormed using a proprietary wormer. It is advantageous to treat the flock as if it had Blackhead and Coccidiosis. Additionally all birds should be caught and thoroughly dusted with a louse powder against feather mites and lice.

A good plan during February is to test any incubator that is to be used during the season, using bantam eggs, to check that it is functioning perfectly.

Broodiness in hens

Hens do not go broody overnight. Some pheasants start to lay in mid-March and it is necessary to plan to have broody hens ready by that time which takes planning and management. Hens are reluctant to go broody on nothing, so at the beginning of March some eggs should be left each day in one or two nest boxes. To ensure that they are not allowed to become too stale for eating purposes it is wise to mark them with the date and change them every three days. There are other ways too of encouraging broodiness and one simple way is to reduce the pellets in their feed and increase the grain content.

Construction of nest boxes is important and a good tip is to build a tunnel leading into the nest box making it fairly dark and cosy. For some reason the hens like this and tend to crowd into it which in itself seems to encourage broodiness in each other.

Beware of sick hens

There is one important point to bear in mind. Sickness or a debilitated condition can make a hen go broody so always check them over and satisfy yourself that they are in good health before setting them on eggs.

Preparation of Breeding stock

In the same way that a bantam flock requires pre-breeding season attention so too does adult pheasant stock. February is a good month to treat for Fowl Pest. It is economic to carry this out when treating your bantam flock if you have one. As with the bantams, it is a good month to treat all stock with a wormer as unless really necessary these should be avoided during the laying season as there is a tendency for them to put birds off the lay for a day or two.

Nesting cover

Pheasants do not like to nest in the open, their natural tendency is to make a nest scrape in a dark quiet corner. Unless the aviaries are well planted with natural cover, additional material should be put in suitable corners during the first week of March. Suitable branches can be obtained from several species of Conifer, such as Scots Pine, Douglas Fir, Norway Spruce and *Cupressocyparis leylandii.*

Nesting boxes

In general most pheasants make nest scrapes on the ground but surprisingly most species can be persuaded to use nest boxes. Early March is the correct time to put these out in the aviaries and ensure they have a layer of straw in the bottom. A good tip is to put a few inches of sand in first as this helps the hen to make a nest of suitable shape. The nest boxes themselves should be about 18″ (46cm) long and of 12″ × 12″ (30 × 30cm) cross section with a lip to the open end of about 3 – 4 inches (8 – 10cm) to retain the sand and straw. The boxes should be fixed a few inches off the ground with 4½″ (11cm) bricks underneath them.

Sand under the straw makes the shaping of the nest easy. The number of eggs in a clutch should depend on their size.

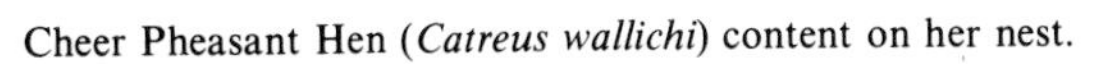

Cheer Pheasant Hen (*Catreus wallichi*) content on her nest.

Feeding in the pre-breeding season

February is the month in which to change the pheasant's diet from a winter ration of maintenance pellets onto a breeders ration which has a higher protein and vitamin content. This change should start at the beginning of February and as the month progresses it is wise to increase the pellet ration and decrease the wheat content of the daily feed.

Laying seasons in captivity

When can the first eggs be expected? This is always a difficult question influenced by so many factors including, of course, the health of the birds. Leaving aside special techniques such as the use of artificial light, the principle factors affecting first laying dates are hours of daylight, the weather, the age of the stock and feed quality. Surprisingly the weather does not affect laying as much as might be expected since pheasants along with other birds have their instincts

Cock Grey Peacock Pheasant (*Polyplectron bicalcaratum*) displaying to its mate. Note the pop-hole into the shelter behind.

principally triggered off by the length of the day; that is the hours of daylight, rather than whether the day is sunny or not. An unusually cold spell will however retard laying and a sunless Spring may lead to a late season and poor fertility. Poor quality food will also retard laying as will too late a transfer onto breeder rations.

The other factor, age of stock, is much simpler. In general first year birds seem to lay between one and two weeks later than mature birds and will usually be less prolific. The following table gives approximate dates when first eggs can be expected of some of the more common species. It also gives the number of days that the eggs of each species take to hatch – a subject that will be referred to in the next section.

Golden	end March	22 days
Silver	mid March	25 days
Lady Amherst	early April	22 days
Reeves	early April	25 days
Mikado	early April	27 days
Elliot's	mid March	25 days
Hume's	early April	27 days
Swinhoe's	mid March	25 days
Cheer	mid April	26 days
Monal	early April	28 days
Grey Peacock-Pheasant	wide variation	22 days
Red Junglefowl	early March	19 – 21 days
Grey Junglefowl	April	21 – 22 days
Koklass	April	26 – 27 days
Kalij	mid April	25 days
Blue Eared-Pheasant	end April	26 – 28 days
Brown Eared-Pheasant	end April	26 days
Siamese Fireback	end April	24 days

Incubation periods

As can be seen from the table there is a wide variation in the number of days that the eggs of different species take to incubate. This can cause problems although they are not as great as may at first appear. On the whole, chicks of different species get on perfectly well together – indeed experience indicates that mixing of species can be beneficial when rearing under brooder lamps. Different species have slightly varying feeding patterns and competition for food seems to stimulate the less enthusiastic feeders – stimulation which is normally provided by the clucking, pecking and scraping of the hen bird.

Keeping records

Where incubators only are being used it is important to clearly mark all eggs with the date of hatch expected and to keep good records of setting and expected hatching dates. With broody hens it is a little more difficult because it is essential that all eggs under one hen are due to hatch within a day or so of each other. However, with a little thought and care it is quite easy to make up a clutch of several different species.

The following example illustrates the point.

Day one:	Set two Monal eggs–due 28 days later
Day two:	Nil
Day three:	Set one Cheer egg–due 26 days later
Day four:	Set two Elliot's eggs–due 25 days later + two Silver eggs–due 25 days later
Day five:	Nil
Day six:	Nil
Day seven:	Set two Grey Junglefowl eggs–due 21 days later
Day eight:	Set two Red Junglefowl eggs–due 22 days later

Clutch complete: eleven eggs.

Many breeders take the clutch of eggs away from a broody hen three days before hatching and transfer them to a still air hatcher and then set a second clutch of eggs under the hen. If short of broody hens this is worth doing but a careful watch should be made each day for signs that a hen subjected to a long stint on the nest is not getting restive and 'going off' being broody.

Egg eating

This can be a serious problem which is almost certainly peculiar to captive conditions. With some pairs of birds it never occurs, with others once started it never stops. It arises with certain species more than others.

The basic cause is usually lack of nesting cover, but after several eggs have been collected some hens get bored and seem to lay their eggs

Cock Silver Pheasant (*Lophura nycthemera*) displaying inflated wattles during the breeding season.

anywhere regardless of how much nesting cover there may be. Egg eating is probably started by the birds tapping at the new object – the egg – in their aviary. Usually it is started by the cock bird. Generally the egg breaks, particularly if it is from one of the species that lay weak shelled eggs and once this has happened it is found to be good to eat and the trouble starts.

How can it be stopped? Every aviculturist has his pet methods, some of which work – for a time at any rate. The most effective, if it is possible, is to separate the cock and hen each day. I have a pair of White Eared-Pheasants of which the cock bird is and always has been an inveterate egg eater. Almost all eggs are obtained by putting the cock with the hen on the day she is not due to lay and separating them the following day when she is. The hen generally lays on alternate days and the eggs from this pair have always been fertile.

More subtle cures are tried, such as mixing mustard, tabasco and other 'hot' spices into an egg but these seldom work and indeed some birds seem to prefer their eggs doctored. More effective is de-beaking of the offending bird but the effect sometimes only lasts for a few days until the top mandible is no longer tender.

Egg collection and storage

Almost all breeders take all eggs away from the parent birds and hatch them under a hen or in an incubator. A few leave the second clutch to the parent bird and a very few, usually those who are not really interested in breeding the maximum number possible, leave the eggs to the parent pheasants themselves. With certain species the latter works well up to the time of hatching – then the problems start with baby chicks who get through pen netting or are attacked by the cock bird. It is not on the whole a practice to be recommended if optimum results are to be achieved.

If it is intended to use either an incubator or a broody hen to incubate eggs, then collection once a day in normal weather or twice a day in a very hot spell is recommended. Once collected careful storage of the eggs until they are 'set' is most important. In hot weather eggs need to evaporate moisture in order to keep cool. If the egg temperature exceeds 72° F the egg starts to germinate. If not set it will cool at night and the germ will die. The shell of eggs works rather like the old-fashioned earthenware dishes for keeping butter or milk cool – that is by evaporating water. For this reason eggs should be stored in a cool damp place. Preference is for storage on the ground in a simple storage box. This can be made from a rectangle of bricks with a 3′ × 2′ (91 × 61cm) open space within them. The bricks should be laid on fine mesh wire netting of 3′9″ × 2′9″ (114 × 84cm) size or more which ensures that mice and rats are excluded. The bricks should be two layers high. Two or three inches of clean sand should be laid within the 3′ × 2′ (91 × 61cm) rectangle and a lid of exterior plywood or other suitable material is then fitted over the top.

Eggs should be marked on collection with date, pen number and species so that they can be identified later. In general, if incubators are being used the sooner the eggs are set the better. However for hatching under broodies the storage time appears to be less critical and three days is perfectly satisfactory and if necessary eggs can be stored for a week without much deterioration in fertility. If stored for more than a day the eggs should be turned each day. When placed on the sand for storage the point of the egg should be slightly downward.

Handling of broodies

For those using broody hens for incubation it is important to plan in advance. If a hen appears to be going nicely broody she can often be

Eggs being stored on sand prior to setting. Note wire netting and hinged lid to prevent rats digging their way in.

put off by bad handling in transferring her from her nest box in the henhouse to the one where she is to incubate the pheasant eggs. Similarly bad handling during the weeks of incubation can unsettle the hen.

It helps to have well designed nest boxes and runs for daily feeding and watering. One of the best systems is to use conventional nest boxes with the back cut out and a sliding door in its place. When raised this door opens into a small 2′ × 1′ (61 × 30cm) run with a raised weldmesh base or just sand on the ground. At feeding time each day, which should always be at the same time, all that is needed is to raise the sliding door and usually the hen will pop out into her run for food and water which are placed in it. Sometimes a little encouragement is needed but the hens learn very quickly. Where a row of nest boxes has been used a length of PVC guttering can be run through the small runs to simplify watering.

Broodies should be allowed off the nest for around ten minutes each day – after a few days of 'training' they will normally return to their nest automatically. It is wise however to shut the broodies back into their nest box each day after feeding.

Setting a broody

Transferring a potential broody from henhouse to nest box is a critical moment. First of all it is most important to allow hens a number of days to settle down in the henhouse. Careful note should be made when a hen starts to sit and some eggs should be left under her. After several days the time comes to transfer to the nest box.

Preparation of the nest in the box is important. A lining of about 3″ (8cm) of sand with straw on top makes it easy to hollow out a nest scrape so that eggs will naturally tend to roll into the centre. Transference should always be done as near to dusk as possible when the hens are settling naturally. First take the eggs, say four or five, from under the hen and put them in the nest box. Next very quietly and gently lift the hen from her nest in the henhouse and carry her to wherever the nest box is located – preferably near to the henhouse. Shut her in and leave her quietly for the night. The less fuss and flurry the better. Hopefully the hen will settle down. It is wise to leave her on her eggs for two or three days to be sure she has settled before substituting a clutch of pheasant eggs.

Setting of eggs

The fresher the eggs are the better as it is a proven fact that such eggs have a slightly stronger germ than those which are several days old, and this seems to make a considerable difference when incubator hatching. If it is intended to rely on incubators the eggs should be set soon after collection. The temptation to wait until there is a full clutch before setting should be resisted.

With broody hens a delay of four to five days seems to make little difference except with species that are suffering from poor fertility due to in-breeding. It is best to substitute the pheasant eggs while the bird is off the nest feeding or last thing at night. If a clutch is being made up from eggs of several species and perhaps there is only one 28 day (see page 46) incubation period egg, then it is wise to leave all or most of the hen eggs until the quantity of pheasant eggs under her number at least four.

Egg candling

A number of infertile eggs in a clutch can seriously affect the chances of hatching some or all of the remainder. The reason for this is that after a certain stage the chick forming within the egg starts to generate its own additional heat – obviously an infertile egg does not do this resulting in the temperature of the adjacent eggs being lower than they should be.

For this reason and also that of the desire to know as soon as possible if fertile eggs are being produced most breeders 'candle' their eggs. Candling is the name given to shining a bright light through an egg to see if the forming embryo can be seen. There are proprietary egg candlers on the market, but many people make their own. All that is required is a light bulb, lamp fitting, switch, flex and a tin can or small wooden box with a hole of about 1″ (2.5cm) diameter in its side. The lamp fitting is fixed inside the box, the bulb inserted and the light switched on. The egg to be candled is held against the 1″ (2.5cm) diameter hole in a darkened room. A forming embryo can be detected in most light shelled eggs from about four days after incubation has commenced. Dud eggs should be removed, but if in doubt always wait an extra few days and check again.

Another advantage of candling is that the size of the air cell inside the

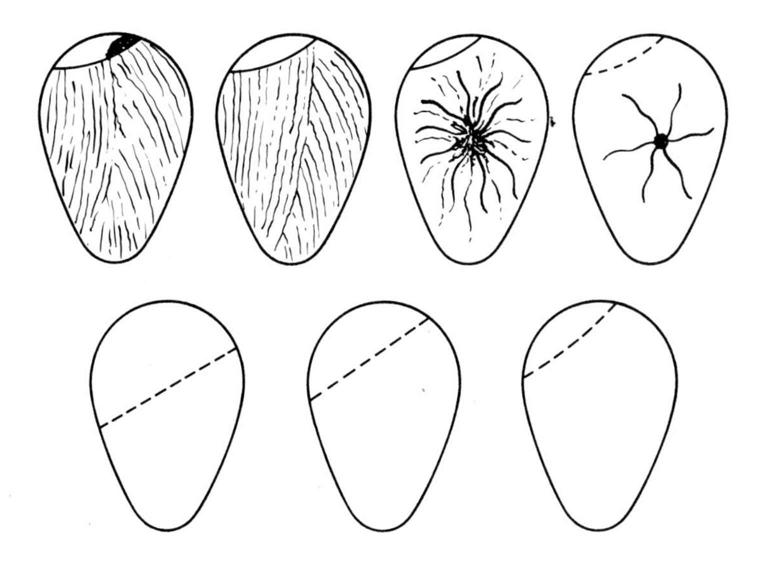

Stages of embryo and air sac development – the rate of the latter is dependent on the hatching period for the egg. Stage one can normally be seen after 3 – 4 days of incubation.

egg can be seen. For incubator hatching this is most important as it can provide a guide as to whether the humidity is too high or too low. Eggs should finish just before hatching with an air cell of approximately one-third of the egg volume. More than this indicates too low humidity, and less too high humidity.

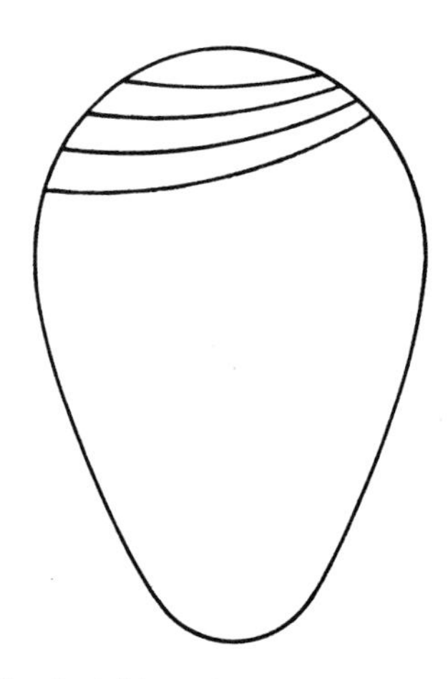

Air sac development. Each sac represents approximately 25% of incubation period.

The hatching stage

The hatching stage is the moment of truth – and always an exciting one. When hatching is in process in a still air incubator many of which have clear dome tops the important rule to remember is not to interfere. Every time the lid is lifted to take a closer look the humidity will drop, and high humidity at the hatching stage is an important element in successful hatching. There is a great temptation also to feel that the 'poor little chicks' must be hungry and take them from the incubator too soon. In fact, chicks are all the better for spending the first twenty-four hours after hatching resting in the incubator. When hatching under broody hens there are three different procedures. The first has already been mentioned – that of taking the clutch from the hen three days before hatching is due and putting a fresh clutch under her. The first clutch is, of course, put into a hatcher for the final stage.

The second procedure is to allow the hen to hatch the chicks, but then to remove the chicks after hatching and before they leave the nest and start to feed. In this instance it is most unwise to attempt to use the hen for a second clutch. There is no doubt that a few pheasant species, of which the Brown Eared-Pheasant and Sonnerat's Junglefowl are two, seem to hatch better and avoid 'splayed' legs if allowed to hatch under the hen and stay with her for the first 12 – 24 hours. The reason probably is that they remain almost inert under the hen and gain strength slowly (in an incubator chicks are inclined to dash around looking for a hen to get under) and can push up gently under the hen and gradually strengthen the leg muscles.

The third procedure is to allow the hen to keep and brood the chicks herself.

Broody hen with White Eared-Pheasant chicks. *Photo: Paradise Bird Gardens, Hale, Cornwall.*

Rearing under broody hens

This is a more natural method than brooder lamp rearing and has many advantages. There is no risk of people being 'imprinted' on the chicks. Imprinting may well be a reason why fertility in the Brown Eared-Pheasants (most of which seem unnaturally friendly towards man) has dropped off so much in recent years.

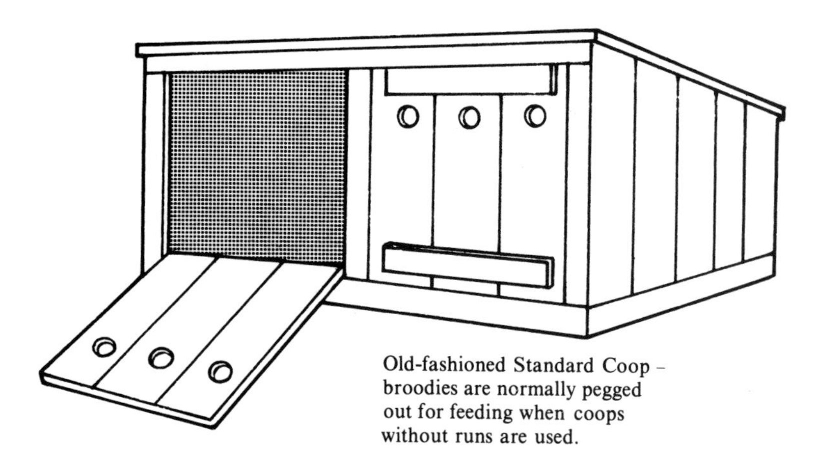

Old-fashioned Standard Coop – broodies are normally pegged out for feeding when coops without runs are used.

There is also no doubt that chicks reared outside in movable coops and runs harden off more quickly and the survivors seem to build up a greater resistance to disease. If this system is adopted then additional precautions with regard to the health of the broody to those recommended earlier are advisable.

Whilst the broody is sitting on the eggs and is coming off the nest just once each day for food and water in individual dishes is an easy time for additional precautionary treatment. Wormer in the drinking water is a simple matter and a five-day treatment with a broad spectrum antibiotic such as Terramycin is also advisable. Additionally it is wise to ensure that the nest box is well dusted with a louse powder so that any remaining feather lice or mites are removed during the incubation period.

The critical time with broody hen rearing is the transfer from nest box to coop and run. This is best done in the middle of the day. The hen should be put gently into the coop with the front of the coop shut. An old sack makes an ideal flat dry base to the coop. The chicks should be transferred and the hen will usually call them to her.

The chicks should be continuously put back under the hen until they are all settled. It is wise to check every quarter of an hour or so to see that all the chicks are settled and that one is not huddled in a corner. Once the chicks have settled with the hen for an hour or two the front of the coop can be removed, but it is wise to block off all but a foot or so of

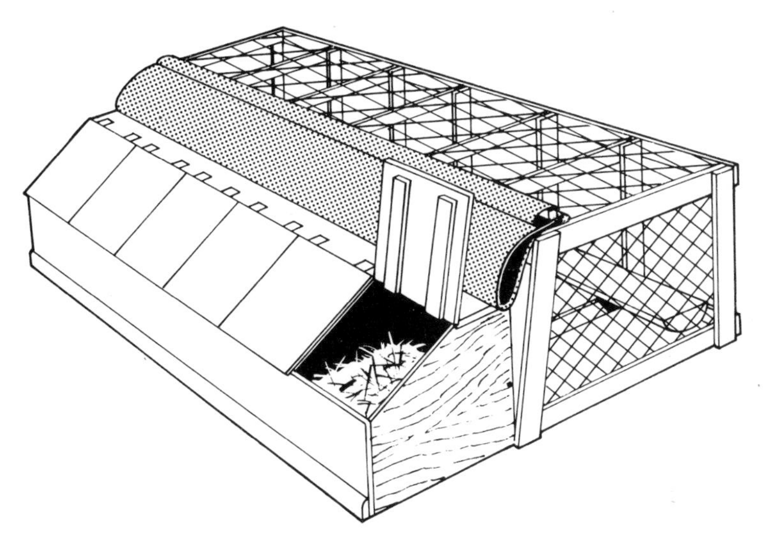

Labour saving coop and run design – note the guttering for water and also the black polythene cover for the coop, which both waterproofs and keeps the coop cool in hot weather.

the run so that the very young chicks cannot get lost at the far end of the run. It should be remembered that the hen is behind the bars of the coop and cannot go to the aid of a lost chick, and pheasant chicks can be remarkably stupid.

A feed of chick crumbs should be put in a shallow dish just inside the run where the hen can reach them but not scratch them all over the place. Water should be in a shallow dish or water-fountain. In either case pebbles should be used to largely fill the dish so that a baby chick cannot be accidentally drowned.

Nowadays more and more breeders are switching to incubators and in so doing are perhaps missing something. In particular they are missing a further great advantage of a good broody bantam when and if they graduate to Peacock-Pheasants. The chicks of the Peacock-Pheasants are always fed by the mother bird finding and picking up insects repeatedly until the chicks eat them. Usually the youngsters will take the insect from the hen's bill. It can take much time and patience with a pair of tweezers to simulate what nature does so simply and efficiently.

Some disadvantages of broodies

Having highlighted the advantages of broody hens there is no doubt that there are risks of disease transference from foster mother to chick. There is no doubt too that broodies do misbehave during incubation due to one of a number of reasons. Thunder, a fright, field mice, a change of weather or disease can all abruptly terminate a broody's desire to sit on the clutch of eggs. Provided there is another broody ready or an incubator is available, do not despair even if a hen is found standing up or even dead on a cold clutch of eggs. The chicks inside an egg can survive for a remarkably long period even when apparently stone cold, so transfer the eggs quickly to the incubator or spare hen and hope that it is not too late. Sometimes all the eggs will survive even though hatching may be delayed 12 – 24 hours.

Management of broody hens at all stages takes time and considerably more trouble than incubators, but is worth while. My strong preference is for broody hatching and brooder lamp rearing.

Black heat infra red lamp of 150 watts used for brooding chicks. The plastic pipe leads to an automatic drinker.

Brooder lamps

There are several types of brooder lamps and they can be heated either by gas or electricity. The electric ones are by far the most convenient for small numbers but numerous batches of chicks. They are usually available with infra red bulbs giving out a warm red glow or an infra red black heat emitter with no light, only heat. The latter are to be recommended providing the shed in which they are fitted is well illuminated.

A black heat emitter of 150 watts will provide quite enough heat for up to fifty chicks, so they are very economical. Ideally they should be suspended over a circle of about two feet in diameter or in a rectangular small pen about 2′ × 3′ (61 × 91cm). Do remember that when first putting chicks under a lamp they have no way of recognising the lamp as their foster mother. A pheasant chick is a timid creature and liable to huddle away in a corner until it learns to recognise the life-giving heat of the lamp. Thus, a small circular enclosure has advantages as the chicks cannot move far from the heat source.

Brooding temperature

The temperature at ground level of the lamps can be adjusted by raising or lowering the lamp. On hatching, a temperature of around 100° F is ideal and this can in theory be dropped by one degree per day. If the heat is too great chicks will get as far from the lamp as possible whilst if it is too low they will constantly crane upwards towards the heat source.

Base material for brooder rearing

There are many different opinions as to what makes the perfect base for baby chicks. Some prefer wood shavings, some pebbles, some sand, some kitchen paper and others, myself included, peat – for the first few days anyway. Peat has the advantage that it provides a dark background to the light coloured chick crumbs. Pheasant chicks being inquisitive always tend to peck at a white spot on a dark background so in addition to a dish of chick crumbs, it is wise to sprinkle a few around on the peat. They soon learn that the crumbs are edible. The peat is easily cleaned out when finished with and will be popular on the kitchen garden.

If wood shavings are used then do make absolutely certain that they have not originated from timber that has been treated against termites as this can poison the chicks if they eat it. If shavings or other light-coloured base material is being used then a good chick crumb dispenser for the first few days is an egg tray of papier-maché. A chick pecking at the crumbs on it makes a tapping sound that intrigues the other chicks and stimulates the desire to feed.

Chicks can be reared on peat – it contrasts well against the feed – note that several species are being reared together, including Sonnerat's, Satyr, Tragopan and Mikado.

Most pheasant chicks start to feed very easily but some species are more difficult than others. There are several tricks for over-coming the problem, the commonest and simplest of which is to include one or two bantam or game pheasant chicks with each clutch of eggs as these always start feeding easily. Chicks are like children, they follow the example of others. If mixed batches of chicks are being made up then difficulties with getting chicks to start feeding are unlikely. However, do beware with two species – these are the Reeves and

The author's first White Eared-Pheasant chick.

White Eared as both are liable to be very belligerent towards their own species as well as others. The latter strangely enough are quarrelsome for the first day or two then seem to settle down, but the former can be quarrelsome at any time.

Rearing under a brooder lamp in a shed tends to be very simple and is usually disease free. The most common ailment is a blocked anus due to droppings collecting on the immature feathers around it. Symptoms to look for are a chick suddenly going off its food and looking a little mopey. The problem if caught in time is usually easily resolved and once the blockage is removed the chick will normally recommence feeding.

Rearing shed

It is in chick-rearing methods that one tends to change techniques most – particularly as a collection grows in size. It has been my practice to make management in terms of feeding and watering as

Cock Palawan Peacock-Pheasant (*Polyplectron emphanum*) displaying with tidbit to hen.

quick and simple as possible in order to allow more time for looking slowly and carefully at the chicks themselves. My management development was as follows:

In years one and two, all rearing was done with broody hens, coops and runs. In the third year, a small number of brooder lamps were used suspended over circles of hardboard. The latter worked well until 3 – 4 weeks of age was reached – at this stage chicks flew in all directions every time one tried to feed them. As a result a permanent rearing shed was planned with every consideration catered for. Thirty miniature runs were built 3′ × 2′ (91 × 61cm) in a 30′ × 10′ (9 × 3m) shed with fifteen pens on the concrete base and fifteen above them 4′ (1.2m) higher. Each pen had a door the height of the pen and 2′ (61cm) wide, with a small 9″ × 9″ (23 × 23cm) door in it for feeding. The purpose of the large doors was to make cleaning out the pens easy and they were fitted flush with the base of the pens. Another 9″ × 9″ (23 × 23cm) door was fitted between each pen so that by emptying chicks from one pen only, those next door could be moved in for cleaning without having to handle the chicks, and so on down the line.

In year four broody hens were used in the rearing shed inside the small 3′ × 2′ (91 × 61cm) pens. In the main this was successful but enteritis problems were found in two broods.

In year five all chicks were taken from the hens 12 – 24 hours after hatching and reared under lamps in the shed. No hens therefore came into the shed at all and the chicks remained free from disease.

In subsequent years the same techniques were continued although with more and more eggs taken prior to hatching, finished off in the incubator and second clutches put under the broody hens.

Minor problems have been experienced with dust from the peat used causing a form of sinusitis and swollen eyes in a few chicks. For this reason raised weldmesh floors have been fitted to half the pens. Certainly this will cure the dust problem but it may produce others – time will tell.

An automatic watering system has now been installed which saves hours of work in filling and cleaning little water fountains. Proper chick crumb hoppers, rather than dishes, are used which only have to be filled up about twice each week. All this allows more time to be devoted to the chicks.

Golden Pheasant (*Chrysolophus pictus*) displaying to its mate.

Special feeds

Artificial rearing in a shed is all very well for the aviculturist but it leads to a pretty dull life for the pheasant chick with only chick crumbs to eat, and each other rather than insects to chase. For this reason additional rations given once or twice each day are recommended. Chicks like, and in my opinion need, green food. Lettuce is always popular but of little nutritional value, Chickweed which costs nothing is very popular, as is specially grown alfalfa. The latter is usually fed in the dishes in which it is grown after about five days. Chickweed and lettuce are chopped and mixed with a number of minced hard-boiled eggs – the shells are not removed unless waterglass eggs stored from the previous winter are being used. Millet, small seeds and a vitamin additive SA 37 are included in this 'egg salad', as well as some chick crumbs. The reason for the latter is that the egg salad is almost too popular and is waited for, resulting in less chick crumbs being consumed in certain cases. Some breeders also provide one of the proprietary brands of mixed feeds made up for insectiverous foreign birds.

Insect food

Live insect food is not a necessity for most pheasant species though few refuse it. However chicks of the small Peacock-Pheasants, such as the Palawan and Himalayan Grey Peacock-Pheasants, do need small mealworms or clean maggots to encourage them to start feeding. Just occasionally insects are required to persuade a particularly difficult chick of other species to feed.

Feather pecking

The main problem likely to arise with artificial rearing during the period prior to putting the chicks outside, usually at around five weeks of age, is feather pecking. This is a problem brought about by boredom and artificial conditions and it is important to spot it early and act quickly. It takes the form, during the first four weeks, of pecking the feathers off the backs of each other and along the wing coverts but is easily cured. If caught at an early stage it is usually sufficient to clip with scissors, nail clippers or small wire cutters, the last $\frac{1}{16}$" – $\frac{1}{8}$" (1.6 – 3mm) off the top mandible. If this does not cure the problem then the fitting of plastic 'bits' is recommended. These are available in three sizes of which the middle size is the most

Standard 10′ × 5′ (3 × 1.5m) sections are quick to erect for young poults. Roofing with PVC sheeting eliminates risk of losses from summer thunderstorms.

useful. They are obtainable through most game farmers and come with fitting instructions.

Reducing heat

Usually feather pecking begins at four to five weeks of age which is just when chicks are reaching the poult stage. Heat should have been steadily reduced during the first three to four weeks, and then turned off altogether. A week in the shed without heat before moving young birds outside is advisable – it is obvious too that a sudden cold, wet spell is not a good time to move birds out.

Poult pens

There is little point in lavishing love and care on chicks and then putting them out into open-topped pens in which they will die of Pneumonia during the first June thunderstorm. For this reason a fully roofed outside pen is recommended. It need not be large, and indeed a large number of small pens makes for much easier management. Too often breeders do a grand job of rearing chicks only to lose them through unsuitable and insufficient accommodation once they have grown to six weeks or over.

Small pens of around 10′ × 3′ (3 × 1m) roofed over with corrugated PVC sheeting make ideal units. They can be very quickly put up using standard sections 10′ × 5′ (3 × 1.5m) with or without gates. These are available from or through a number of pheasant game farmers. A base of 4″ – 6″ (10 – 15cm) of sharp sand is strongly recommended as it remains clean and can easily be disinfected after the end of one breeding season, ready for the next.

Wing tagging

There are two principle methods of marking young birds – leg rings and wing tags. The former can catch in the growing spurs of young cock birds and therefore the preference is for wing tags. These can be bought already consecutively numbered.

Sexing of chicks and poults

This is a subject which could fill a book on its own, indeed there is a good little booklet on just this subject by the American aviculturist, Lloyl Stromberg. In the main it is a question of experience. Space does not permit the sort of detailed descriptions that would be necessary to cover all the species. However, it can be said that spur growth is usually a good indication of cock birds and provided there are both cock and hen poults their sexes are usually obvious by comparison with each other by around fourteen weeks of age.

The season's end

The breeding season does not end with the last egg laid or the last chick reared. Successful breeding stock is valuable and should be cared for. For the hen bird in particular the breeding season is a physical strain particularly under captive conditions where collection of eggs normally induces an abnormally long laying season and far more eggs than would be laid in the wild.

Egg production is closely followed by the moult which again puts a physical strain on the bird. Once egg production ceases around mid-June, a repeat of the pre-breeding season routine is recommended. That is to treat all birds with a proprietary wormer and it is a good idea to follow this with a day or two of added vitamins.

A month later the last of the chicks should be hatched and this is a good time to treat all your stock once more with a live vaccine treatment against fowl pest.

Chapter 7

THE PHEASANT SPECIES

Introduction

This chapter describes briefly the forty-eight pheasant species. It has been based upon that outstanding work on pheasants – '*The Pheasants of the World*' by Dr Jean Delacour. I have deliberately followed the species sequence used by Dr Delacour for ease of reference and would like to express my special thanks to him for permission to do this. I hope that many readers of this book will graduate to his fine work in due course.

Where species are endangered these are indicated thus ⚠E. It must be noted that in the following classification Rheinartia is corrected from the original Rheinardia and that several suffixes to the specific names are not as in the original descriptions (e.g. . . . i for . . . ii).

Note: Limitation of space has precluded feather by feather description of the birds. Where possible photographs have been used, but where these were not available comparisons or general descriptions have been included. General reference has been made only to the nominate race of each species. Approximate numbers in captivity have been based upon the World Pheasant Association's census of 1976.

Order *GALLIFORMES*
Family *Phasianidae* Sub-family *Phasianinae*

THE BLOOD PHEASANTS Genus - *Ithaginis*

The Blood Pheasants are the least pheasant-like of all the genera, more resembling partridges in shape and size. They form one species *Ithaginis cruentus* (Hardwicke) 1821, with fourteen sub-species. At present they are uncommon in captivity, the only major group being in Major Iain Grahame's collection at Daws Hall in Suffolk. The main variations between cock birds of the different sub-species lie in the amount of red on the breast and the amount of red and black around the forehead and throat. Cock birds have a distinct crest on the head. Hens are broadly similar and of mottled brown.

Cock Blood Pheasant (*Ithaginus cruentus*) at Daws Hall Wildlife Farm where the first captive breeding took place.

Distribution is from Nepal throughout Tibet and Northern Burma to north-west China. They normally live between 11,000 feet (3,300m) and 15,000 feet (4,500m) in summer, moving down to around 9,000 feet (2,700m) in winter.

Avicultural Notes

Recommended aviary size	150 square feet (14sq.m) with sand base
Number in captivity	Approximately 25
Full adult plumage	First year
Egg clutch size	5 – 12 eggs
Incubation period	27 – 29 days
Feeding habits	Primarily vegetarian with emphasis on green food (grass) and fruit
Special note	One of the more difficult species to rear in captivity

THE TRAGOPAN PHEASANTS Genus - *Tragopan*

Western Tragopan - *Tragopan melanocephalus* (J. E. Gray) 1829 Ⓔ

This is probably the rarest of all the Tragopan with, it is believed, only one specimen (a hen) in captivity anywhere in the world. They come from the Western end of the Himalayas and have recently been recorded in Swat Kohistan and Azad Kashmir. Formerly they inhabited much of Hazara and spread east through Kashmir to Garhwal in India which borders onto the range of the Satyr Tragopan.

The Western Tragopan is similar in size to the better-known Satyr Tragopan but is much darker in general colouring with the exception of its head and chest which are well illustrated on the next page. The hen bird is similar to the Satyr Tragopan hen but is darker. Its normal altitude range is 8,000 - 10,000 feet (2,400 - 3,000m).

Avicultural Notes

Recommended aviary size	400 square feet (37sq.m)
Number in captivity	1
Full adult plumage	Second year
Egg clutch size	Unknown, but probably 3 - 4
Incubation period	28 days
Feeding habits	Largely vegetarian with emphasis on fruit and berries

Cock Western Tragopan (*Tragopan melanocephalus*) photographed in a Lahore garden by Mr C. Savage.

Cock Western Tragopan, a rare sight, photographed in Pakistan.

Satyr Tragopan – *Tragopan satyra* (Linnaeus) 1758

The most common of all the Tragopans, both in captivity and in the wild. The Satyr is probably every pheasant aviculturist's dream with its lovely crimson feathering interspersed in the case of the adult cock bird with white ocelli which start small near the neck and become larger farther back towards the tail. The wonderful sight of a Satyr cock with lappets down and horns erect is quite unbelievable.

Its range is from Kumaon in India eastwards through Nepal, Sikkim and Bhutan at least as far as Nyan Jang Chu. It normally lives around 8,000 – 10,000 feet (2,400 – 3,000m) moving down to around 4,000 feet (1,200m) in winter. It lives in the thickly-forested mountain areas.

Avicultural Notes

Recommended aviary size	400 square feet (37sq.m) with grass base
Number in captivity	350
Full adult plumage	Second year
Egg clutch size	2 – 4 eggs
Incubation period	28 days
Feeding habits	Largely vegetarian with emphasis on fruit and berries

Cock Satyr Tragopan showing off to the author's wife. Note the silver tag on the left wing for record purposes.

Blyth's Tragopan – *Tragopan blythi blythi* (Jerdon) 1870 (E)

The only specimens now in captivity are at the small zoo at Kohima in Nagaland in North-east India.

The principal difference between this bird and the Temmincks Tragopan which borders onto its territory is the dramatic golden yellow facial colouring. The chest feathering too is very much greyer.

There is a sub-species, the Molesworth's Tragopan, *Tragopan blythi molesworthi.*

Avicultural Notes

Recommended aviary size	400 square feet (37sq.m) with grass base
Number in captivity	9
Full adult plumage	Second year
Egg clutch size	2 – 4 eggs
Incubation period	28 days
Feeding habits	Primarily vegetarian with emphasis on fruit and berries

Temminck's Tragopan – *Tragopan temmincki* (J. E. Gray) 1831

At one time the Temminck's Tragopan was the most common of the genus in captivity and was bred fairly prolifically and was found to live to a good age. Thought by many to be the most beautiful of the Tragopans they are nearest in colouring to the Satyr although the bright red of the Satyr is replaced by a deeper red colouring. The ocelli on the chest of the Satyr are replaced by much larger patches of a pinkish-grey as opposed to the white markings. The facial skin is a vivid blue and, as with the other Tragopans when displaying, lappets and inflated skin horns are striking.

The hen bird, although darker, is much like the Satyr hen and this has led, in America in particular, to cross-breeding with the Satyr. Much of the stock is now seriously inbred and proving harder to propagate each year. Very few now remain in England and other parts of Europe. They have the largest distribution area of any of the Tragopans and live at similar altitudes to the other species in the group. Their distribution is from north-eastern Assam and Burma through south-eastern Tibet and then east to Yunnan, Szechuan, Shensi and Hupeh and South to the extreme north-western part of Tonkin. The Temminck's is illustrated on page 28.

Avicultural Notes

Recommended aviary size	400 square feet (37sq.m) with grass base
Number in captivity	200
Full adult plumage	Second year
Egg clutch size	7 – 8 eggs
Incubation period	28 days
Feeding habits	Primarily vegetarian with emphasis on fruit and berries

Cabot's Tragopan – *Tragopan caboti* (Gould) 1857 Ⓔ

Found only in south-eastern China in the mountain forests of Fokien and Kwangtung, these are by far the most easterly in distribution of all the Tragopans. Whilst they were quite common in collections prior to the First World War, this species is now rare in captivity. The Pheasant Trust at Great Witchingham in Norfolk had a small breeding nucleus based on birds sent over by Dr K. Searle from Hong Kong. These were distributed during 1977/78 to America, Germany and Belgium. They are similar to the Blyth's Tragopan although with more orange coloured facial markings, buff coloured ocelli and plain buff colouring to the underparts. They appear to live at a lower altitude than the other members of the genus, at around 3,000 – 5,000 feet (900 – 1,500m).

Avicultural Notes

Recommended aviary size	400 square feet (37sq.m) with grass base
Number in captivity	20
Full adult plumage	Second year
Egg clutch size	2 – 4 eggs
Incubation period	28 days
Feeding habits	Primarily vegetarian with emphasis on fruit and berries

THE KOKLASS PHEASANT Genus - *Pucrasia*

There are ten races of *Pucrasia* all belonging to one species *Pucrasia macrolopha* (Lesson) 1829. As with Blood Pheasants and the Tragopans, the Koklass have proved to be one of the pheasant aviculturists most severe challenges and indeed few can really claim to have been successful with them. Fortunately they are still fairly

Cock Koklass with crest erect during the breeding season in a nicely grassed aviary (*see also page 13*).

common over much of their vast range which is from Afghanistan and Pakistan in the west, continuously through northern India to Nepal, north-eastern Tibet and north-eastern China. They are, surprisingly, absent from the Eastern Himalayas. Koklass are among the most beautiful of all the pheasants although in an unflamboyant way – the cock bird, when strutting with crest erect is a fine sight. It may be that the practical solution to the propagation of this species in numbers lies, as with the grouse family, in raising them on wire to prevent parasitic infestation to which they appear to be very prone.

Avicultural Notes

Recommended aviary size	400 square feet (37sq.m) with grass base
Number in captivity	80
Full adult plumage	First year
Egg clutch size	9 – 12 eggs
Incubation period	26 – 27 days
Feeding habits	Primarily vegetarian with emphasis on large volumes of green food, particularly grass and lucerne.

THE MONALS Genus - *Lophophorus*

Only one of the three species of Monal, the Himalayan Monal, is represented in captivity so far as is known at the present time. As space is limited, descriptions of the other two – the Chinese Monal, *Lophophorus lhuysi* Geoffroy St. Hilaire 1866 and Sclater's Monal, *Lophophorus sclateri* Jerdon 1870 – have been omitted. Both are endangered species.

Himalayan Monal – *Lophophorus impeyanus* (Latham) 1790

The Himalayan Monal with its heavy body shape is very different to any of the other pheasant species. The brilliant metallic plumage of greens, blues, blacks and purples more than compensate for its squat, heavy, ugly shape and long curved bill. The latter is designed for digging as is soon apparent if they are kept in too small an aviary. They are tough, hardy birds easily kept even by the beginner. In the wild they have fortunately a wide distribution although numbers have been greatly depleted over the past three decades. As their name suggests, they come from the Himalayas, from eastern Afghanistan continuously through Pakistan, northern India, Nepal and Bhutan to southern Tibet. They live at an altitude of 8,000 – 15,000 feet (2,400 – 4,500m) and are probably found in summer at a higher altitude than any other pheasant.

Avicultural Notes

Recommended aviary size	200 square feet (18.6sq.m) with grass and sand base
Number in captivity	1,250
Full adult plumage	Second year
Egg clutch size	4 – 8 eggs
Incubation period	28 days
Feeding habits	Easily maintained on poultry pellets and grain
Special note	Young birds are hard to sex. The first signs of the cock bird are black mottling below the beak

Immature Himalayan Monal Cock bird. Note the darker feathers growing under the chin which are an aid to sexing this species. The contrast between young bird and adult is clearly shown by comparison with the mature adult shown overleaf.

The beautiful metallic colouring of the Himalayan Monal makes them very desirable birds for any collection. They have the added bonus of being very hardy.

THE JUNGLEFOWLS Genus - *Gallus*

Red Junglefowl – *Gallus gallus* (Linnaeus) 1758

The Red Junglefowl and its five sub-species have proved to be of more importance to man than any other species of bird. They have provided for man all the numerous varieties of domestic fowl that we have today. The original distribution of the Red Junglefowl was from the River Indus in Pakistan on the west through India, eastwards across and down through Malaysia, Java and the Lesser Sunda Islands. They are highly adaptable and can live at altitudes from sea level up to 6,000 feet (1,800m). They resemble, not surprisingly, a barnyard chicken.

As aviary birds they are amenable in every way provided only one cock bird is in each aviary. The cock bird can be run with a number of hens. These Junglefowl can also be kept with other pheasant species, such as Argus or Eared-Pheasant, with which they do not appear to quarrel.

A pair of Red Junglefowl at liberty – it is from this species that all domestic fowl have been bred.

Avicultural Notes

Recommended aviary size	Can be small though due to scratching, grass will not survive in such aviaries
Number in captivity	800
Full adult plumage	First year although improves in the second year
Egg clutch size	8 – 10 eggs
Incubation period	19 – 21 days
Feeding habits	As for poultry

La Fayette's Junglefowl – *Gallus lafayettei* (Lesson) 1831

A fine-looking bird of typical Junglefowl shape, the La Fayette's is distinguished especially in the cock bird by its striking red lappets with a large interior yellow patch.

They come from Sri Lanka and are found from sea level up to 6,000 feet (1,800m) wherever sufficient cover exists. They have been badly neglected in captivity and only in America are there any reasonable numbers.

Avicultural Notes

Recommended aviary size	Can be small
Number in captivity	140
Full adult plumage	Second year
Egg clutch size	2 – 4 eggs
Incubation period	20 – 21 days
Feeding habits	As for poultry

Sonnerat's Junglefowl – *Gallus sonnerati* (Temminck) 1813

Whilst being chicken-like in shape, the Sonnerat's or Grey Junglefowl is particularly distinctive for its cape or neck hackles of almost waxy appearance and feel and whitish-yellow colouring. These feathers were and indeed are still much sought after by fly-tyers for tying many of the most famous trout and salmon flies. Demand led to a dramatic reduction in their numbers and since 1968 all export of the birds and their feathers has been banned from India where they come from the southern part of the country. Their normal altitude range is 2,000 – 5,000 feet (600 – 1,500m).

They are also interesting in that during the summer moult they go into an 'eclipse' plumage during which they lose their long tail feathers and their neck hackles are replaced by short black feathers for about two months. This species is well illustrated on pages 30 and 38.

Avicultural Notes

Recommended aviary size	100 square feet (9.3sq.m) sanded, or 200 square feet with grass base
Number in captivity	400
Full adult plumage	Second year
Egg clutch size	4 – 8 eggs
Incubation period	20 – 21 days
Feeding habits	As for poultry
Special note	Although not requiring heat in winter, a good dry shelter is important. Chicks sometimes need a little extra care and attention in feeding – i.e. mealworms, etc.

Green Junglefowl – *Gallus varius* (Shaw) 1798

Again with typical barnyard-fowl configuration the Green Junglefowl is nevertheless a most striking bird with lovely metallic greeny-black feathering on the cock bird set off by a comb, green near the head passing to mauvish-purple and red on the outer edges.

The Green Junglefowl is the most delicate of the Junglefowl and require some heat in winter. They appear to mix well with other pheasant species.

Avicultural Notes

Recommended aviary size	Can be small
Number in captivity	90
Full adult plumage	First year although improves in second year
Egg clutch size	6 – 10 eggs
Incubation period	21 days
Feeding habits	As for poultry

The Green Junglefowl – colourful but somewhat delicate.

The White Crested Kalij has so much to offer that it is surprising it should have been overlooked by so many aviculturists in the past (*see also photo on page viii*).

A White Crested Kalij cock – attractive and an easy breeder.

THE GALLO PHEASANTS Genus - *Lophura*

The Gallo Pheasants are the largest group or genus of pheasants comprising ten species and numerous sub-species.

Kalij Pheasant – *Lophura leucomelana* (Latham) 1790

This is a large group of pheasants of which the best known in captivity is the Nepal Kalij (*Lophura leucomelana leucomelana*) the nominate race and the White-Crested Kalij (*Lophura leucomelana hamiltoni*). The Kalij Pheasants range from Pakistan in the west across northern India to Nepal and also down into Bangladesh. They like to live in thick forest and have survived well in spite of the ravages to their forest homes. They are hardy and easy to breed and have for too long been neglected by pheasant aviculturists. There are nine sub-species of Kalij. The Black-Breasted Kalij is shown on page 3.

Avicultural Notes

Recommended aviary size	200 square feet (18.6sq.m) on grass base
Number in captivity	1,200 of five sub-species
Full adult plumage	First year
Egg clutch size	9 – 15 eggs
Incubation period	24 – 25 days
Feeding habits	Standard pheasant feed

Silver Pheasant – *Lophura nycthemera* (Linnaeus) 1758

The Silver Pheasant has long been popular with aviculturists as it is a fine looking bird which is hardy and easy to keep under aviary conditions. There are thirteen recognised sub-species all bearing close similarities. Typical cock birds are illustrated on pages 32 and 47. Silver Pheasants come principally from China but their range extends to north-east Burma, central Thailand, Vietnam and south-west Cambodia.

Avicultural Notes

Recommended aviary size	100 – 200 square feet (9.3 – 18.6sq.m)
Number in captivity	2,300
Full adult plumage	Second year
Egg clutch size	4 – 6 eggs
Incubation period	25 – 26 days
Feeding habits	Standard pheasant feed

Imperial Pheasant – *Lophura imperialis* (Delacour & Jabouille) 1924 (E)

Discovered in 1923 by Dr Jean Delacour and his party in Annam, the Imperial Pheasants in captivity are all derived from one pair which reached his home at Clères in 1924. The cock bird was still alive in 1939 but all the stock at Clères was lost in the War. Since then the

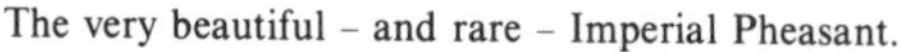
The very beautiful – and rare – Imperial Pheasant.

stock elsewhere virtually died out until, at Antwerp Zoo, a cock bird was crossed with a Silver hen and nineteen chicks resulted. This encouraged a long programme of selective hybridising between 1959 and 1970 resulting in birds which bear every resemblance to the original wild specimens. All these birds are housed at Antwerp Zoo with the exception of one pair and their progeny at London Zoo.

Avicultural Notes

Recommended aviary size	150 square feet (14sq.m)
Number in captivity	30
Full adult plumage	Second year
Egg clutch size	5 – 7 eggs
Incubation period	25 days
Feeding habits	Similar to Edwards'

Edwards' Pheasant – *Lophura edwardsi* (Oustalet) 1896

Originally discovered in 1895 nothing more was heard of them until 1923 when Dr Delacour went on an expedition to central Annam. A number of pairs were trapped and a total of fifteen birds were successfully shipped to Clères where four cocks and three hens were retained and successfully bred from in 1925. Since then they have been widely distributed although in-breeding has led to stock degeneration and infertility. A stud book of this species has been started by the World Pheasant Association. The resultant attention

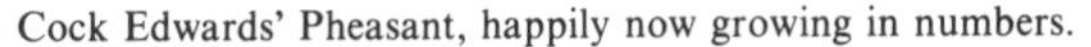

Cock Edwards' Pheasant, happily now growing in numbers.

to the genetics involved is likely to ensure their survival in captivity for many years to come. They are one of the earliest layers.

Avicultural Notes

Recommended aviary size	150 square feet (14sq.m)
Number in captivity	700
Full adult plumage	First year
Egg clutch size	4 – 7 eggs
Incubation period	22 days
Feeding habits	Non-vegetarian; grain and poultry feed

Swinhoe's Pheasant – *Lophura swinhoei* (Gould) 1863 (E)

The most numerous in captivity of all the endangered pheasant species, the Swinhoe's was first discovered by the British Consul (of that name) in Formosa (now Taiwan) in 1862. Baron James de Rothschild paid £250 for the first pair that came to Europe in 1866. These so successfully produced offspring that by 1870 a pair could be obtained for as little as ten pounds. Remarkably the price today (1979) is almost identical to that of a hundred years ago.

The cock birds are most colourful and this species does well in relatively small pens. A good species for the beginner although they do not normally breed in their first season. In Taiwan they live in close canopy forest from sea level to 7,000 feet (2,100m).

Avicultural Notes

Recommended aviary size	150 square feet (14sq.m)
Number in captivity	1,700
Full adult plumage	Second year
Egg clutch size	6 – 12 eggs
Incubation period	25 days
Feeding habits	Standard pheasant diet

Salvadori's Pheasant – *Lophura inornata inornata* (Salvadori) 1879

A rather drab species, the Salvadori's cock bird looks very similar in size, shape and colour to the hen Malay Crestless Fireback with the principal obvious difference being a bright yellow spot behind the eye. The hen is of bright reddish chestnut colouring and is similar in size to the male.

They come from deep mountain forest in West Sumatra. The first record of them is a cock and three hens which arrived at Clères in 1939. They were lost in the War that followed shortly after. Recently pairs have been imported into America and Europe. Messieurs Houpert and Lastère in 1976 became the first to breed from this species. Since then Mr Charles Sivelle has also bred them in America.

Avicultural Notes

Recommended aviary size	150 – 200 square feet (14 – 18.6sq.m)
Number in captivity	10
Full adult plumage	First year
Egg clutch size	2 eggs
Incubation period	22 days
Feeding habits	As for Fireback pheasants
Special note	Some heat in winter advisable

Malay Crestless Fireback – *Lophura erythrophthalma erythrophthalma* (Raffles) 1822

The cock bird is well illustrated in the photograph below whilst its hen, of dark blue overall colouring is as mentioned above very similar to the male Salvadori's Pheasant. These birds fall into the

A fine Malay Crestless Fireback Cock seen with a Chinese Bamboo Partridge.

category of a semi-tropical species coming from the hot low-lying jungles of West Sumatra.

They were first discovered in 1822 but the first recorded breeding was not until 1872 in France. Credit for the first recorded breeding in England is given to Mr Sharpe and Mr Winstanley as recently as 1971. This is a reminder that there are still new worlds to conquer in the field of pheasant aviculture. Numbers in captivity are still very few. There is a Bornean sub-species.

Avicultural Notes

Recommended aviary size	150 square feet (14sq.m)
Number in captivity	65
Full adult plumage	First year, but do not breed until second year
Egg clutch size	3 – 6 eggs
Incubation period	23 – 24 days
Feeding habits	Normal pheasant diet with addition of fresh fruit, mealworms, etc. advisable
Special note	Heat in winter advisable

The Crested Firebacks – *Lophura ignita* (Shaw) 1897

The nominate race of this group of pheasants is the Lesser Bornean Crested Fireback (*Lophura ignita ignita*) which comes from Java and southern Borneo. This group are all semi-tropical species and the Lesser Bornean in particular require some heat to see them safely through the winter months. They are inclined to lay late, particularly in a poor summer and may well be a species that will respond well to artificial lighting to induce early laying.

They are a large-bodied bird with incredible blue wattles on the cock bird which become very prominent when it is excited. The males become tame and sometimes belligerent in captivity. They do not breed until their second or third year. There is also a Greater Bornean Crested Fireback which is very similar.

Rather better known to pheasant aviculturists is the Vieillot's Crested Fireback (*Lophura ignita rufa*) which resembles the Bornean in general shape and size. It is not totally hardy and is difficult to breed successfully in cold climates. Neither species are pheasants for the beginner though there are rather more Viellot's in captivity than Bornean. They come from the lowlands and hills

A magnificent Bornean Crested Fireback – a jewel in any aviary.

of the Malay Peninsular up to Siam in the north and down to Sumatra at the southern end of its range. Like the Bornean, they can be aggressive though this seems directed more towards its mate than to people. (See page 9 for illustration of Vieillot's Fireback.)

It may be wise with both species to keep cock birds separated from their mates until laying commences. They do not appear to breed until their second or third years.

Avicultural Notes

Recommended aviary size	150 – 200 square feet (14 – 18.6sq.m)
Number in captivity	450 of all species
Full adult plumage	First year
Egg clutch size	4 – 8 eggs
Incubation period	24 days
Feeding habits	Standard pheasant diet, plus tidbits of fruit, mealworms, etc.
Special note	Heat necessary in winter

A good study of a hen Siamese Fireback Pheasant.

Cock Siamese Fireback Pheasant displaying to reveal the bright yellow colouring on its back from which the name is derived.

Siamese Fireback – *Lophura diardi* (Bonaparte) 1856

The Siamese Fireback has a large range throughout southern Indo-China where it lives in the bamboo and thick secondary forest from sea level to around 2,000 feet (600m). They make excellent aviary birds and young bred in captivity often become very tame. In bygone days they could be seen free range with their owner's poultry in many parts of Indo-China and Siam. They became known in Europe when the King of Siam sent a pair to the Paris Museum in 1862 and they were first bred in captivity in France in 1866. Although from a warm climate, the Siamese Firebacks are remarkably hardy and tolerant of the sort of winter normally experienced in the United Kingdom. They do, however, require a really good wind-free shelter to ensure their comfort during a cold spell.

They are the first of the Firebacks for the beginner to attempt although they can, and usually do, take three years to mature. However, once mature they breed freely and the sight of the cock bird with red wattles aflame and whirring his wings to show the bright yellow feathering normally hidden by the wing coverts is an ample reward for patience.

Avicultural Notes

Recommended aviary size	150 – 200 square feet (14 – 18.6sq.m)
Number in captivity	400
Full adult plumage	First year although a little duller than in subsequent years
Egg clutch size	5 – 8 eggs
Incubation period	24 – 25 days
Feeding habits	Normal pheasant diet
Special note	Good draught-free shelter or a little heat advised in winter

Bulwer's Wattled Pheasant – *Lophura bulweri* (Sharpe) 1874 (E)

An adult cock Bulwer's Pheasant in display is a most extraordinary sight with his tremendously developed bright blue facial wattles which are not only around the eyes, but are extended in two lobes of up to six inches in length underneath the eyes. At the same time the white tail feathers form an almost complete fan.

Although this species was recorded in 1874 and small numbers have come into captivity from time to time, it was not until 1973 that Dr Estudillo Lopez first bred them. Some were also bred by Mr Charles Sivelle in 1975 but neither pair repeated their success so it would appear that this is a species about which there is still much to learn. The Bulwer's come from the low lying forests of Borneo and on the mountain slopes up to around 2,200 feet (660m). Due to forest destruction they have just been included on the list of endangered species.

Avicultural Notes

Recommended aviary size	200 square feet (18.6sq.m)
Number in captivity	30
Full adult plumage	First year but in an undeveloped form
Egg clutch size	3 – 8 eggs
Incubation period	24 – 26 days
Feeding habits	As for Crested Firebacks
Special note	Heat necessary in winter

THE EARED-PHEASANTS Genus - *Crossoptilon*

Szechuan White Eared-Pheasant – *Crossoptilon crossoptilon crossoptilon* (Hodgson) 1838 (E)

This is the nominate race of the White Eared-Pheasant group, the best known of the other sub-species being the Tibetan *Crossoptilon crossoptilon drouyni* and Dolan's *Crossoptilon crossoptilon dolani.* The first recorded pair in the west arrived at London Zoo in 1891 but did not breed. Some were imported into California in 1935 and a small breeding nucleus built up but by 1970 this had almost died out due probably to in-breeding.

Since then Jersey Zoo has bred well over one hundred from one of two pairs imported via Peking and East Berlin. Others have been imported into America direct from Peking. A reasonable captive stock has now been built up resulting from these importations.

White Eared-Pheasants are striking birds – in fact, unlike the other Eared-Pheasants, they do not have ear tufts. They are large birds with prominent red wattles around the eyes, red legs, and tails of blackish-blue with a metallic sheen. It is the white feathering on the rest of the body however that makes this species so impressive to look at. It also provides the main variation between the sub-species with *c.drouyni* being pure white, *c.dolani* pale grey and the nominate race being white but with grey wings.

White Eared-Pheasants live at high altitudes of 10,000 feet (3,000m) and upwards and come principally from Western Szechuan and Tibet.

Avicultural Notes

Recommended aviary size	200 square feet (18.6 sq.m)
Number in captivity	200
Full adult plumage	First year, but not fertile till second year
Egg clutch size	4 – 7 eggs
Incubation period	24 – 25 days
Feeding habits	Normal pheasant diet but are great diggers

A pair of White Eared-Pheasants. Note lack of ear tufts.

A fine pair of Brown Eared-Pheasants will reward any aviculturalist who adds them to a collection. They are both impressive and amenable.

Brown Eared-Pheasant – *Crossoptilon mantchuricum* (Swinhoe) 1863 Ⓔ

This species can be relied upon to become one of the most friendly and interesting in any collection and is well worth having, although like all the Eared-Pheasants, their digging habits can lead to grassed aviaries looking a little like a badly ploughed field.

Aviculturally they represent an extraordinary success story as all species in captivity are derived from two hens and one cock imported into France in 1864. Since then two more male birds have been imported. Not surprisingly, stock became very in-bred resulting in low fertility. In 1977 a programme of artificial insemination sponsored by the World Pheasant Association showed that the infertility was almost certainly a behavioural not a physical defect problem. Fertility of the first one hundred eggs was over 70 per cent and the experiments proved that A.I. was a practical proposition.

Brown Eared-Pheasants come from Western China where they live in the high altitude forests.

Avicultural Notes

Recommended aviary size	200+ square feet (over 19m)
Number in captivity	870
Full adult plumage	First year but only rarely fertile
Egg clutch size	5 – 8 eggs
Incubation period	26 – 27 days
Feeding habits	Normal pheasant diet but great diggers

Blue Eared-Pheasant – *Crossoptilon auritum* (Pallas) 1811

This is another great favourite with pheasant aviculturists and is, like all the Eared-Pheasants, a most striking bird. It is the most common of this group in captivity and is thought to be still fairly abundant in the wild.

A most attractive Blue Eared-Pheasant. Note the prominent spur denoting cock bird (*see also page 31*).

The Blue Eared is clearly separated from the other two species in distribution and comes from Central Northern China where it occurs over a wide area. Strangely, it was the last of the Eared-Pheasants to come into captivity from China, the first recorded birds being sent to Clères in France in 1929.

Avicultural Notes

Recommended aviary size	200+ square feet (over 19m)
Number in captivity	1,370
Full adult plumage	First year but rarely fertile
Egg clutch size	5 – 8 eggs
Incubation period	26 – 28 days
Feeding habits	Normal pheasant diet but great diggers

THE CHEER PHEASANT Genus - *Catreus*

Cheer Pheasant – *Catreus wallichi* (Hardwicke) 1827 (E)

The Cheer is the only species in this genus and is, in my opinion, one of the most interesting and worthwhile of all the pheasant species. With predominantly grey and golden brown mottled colouring and a

Cock Cheer Pheasant – not the most striking of birds but none the less very worth while keeping. The hen may be seen on page 43.

chunky appearance, they are perhaps one of the drabber species. Nevertheless, in their way they are a very beautiful bird although they can make up in noise when excited for any lack in colour. The Cheer is equipped with a powerful bill and makes good use of it in aviaries and probably in the wild, using it to turn stones. Their range is from Pakistan at the western end through to Nepal at the eastern end and throughout. With the partial exception of Nepal they are becoming rare if not extinct. They normally live at 5,000 – 9,000 feet (1,500m – 2,700m) in open grassy light forest.

Avicultural Notes

Recommended aviary size	200 square feet (18.6sq.m)
Number in captivity	850
Full adult plumage	First year
Egg clutch size	9 – 12 eggs
Incubation period	26 days
Feeding habits	Normal pheasant diet

THE LONG-TAILED PHEASANTS — Genus - *Syrmaticus*

Elliot's Pheasant – *Syrmaticus ellioti* (Swinhoe) 1872 (E)

The Long-tailed Pheasants are among the best of all the pheasants for beginners. All mature in their first year, all are hardy and all lay prolifically in captivity. In spite of this, however, three of the group are listed as endangered in the wild, one of which is the Elliot's from eastern China.

A Cock Elliot's Pheasant – the species are ideal for beginners.

The one problem the aviculturist should watch for with the Elliot's and others of this group is extreme pugnacity of the cock towards its hen or hens. For this reason plenty of shrubs or branches for cover should be put into their aviaries and it is sometimes wise to clip the primary feathers of one wing of the cock bird.

With its whitish-grey neck setting off the red wattles around its eyes, and the metallic golden brown sheen on part of its back feathering, the Elliot's is a most beautiful bird.

Avicultural Notes

Recommended aviary size	200 square feet (18.6sq.m)
Number in captivity	1,550
Full adult plumage	First year
Egg clutch size	6 – 8 eggs
Incubation period	25 days
Feeding habits	Normal pheasant diet

Hume's Bar-tailed Pheasant photographed at Stagsden Bird Gardens. Like all the Long-tailed Pheasants, Hume's can be recommended to the novice.

Hume's Bar-tailed Pheasant – *Syrmaticus humiae humiae* (Hume) 1881 (E)

It was not until 1962 that this species was first bred in captivity. This success was achieved by Mr F. E. B. Johnson who was at that time owner of Stagsden Bird Gardens. Since then they have been bred fairly prolifically until by 1976 there were 876 recorded in captivity. Provided that trouble is taken to avoid in-breeding so far as is possible, numbers should continue to increase.

The Hume's Pheasant lives at 4,000 – 10,000 feet (1,200 – 3,000m) in the mountains of northern Burma and in north-eastern India around the Naga Hills. They are an attractive and colourful pheasant with an intriguing habit of slightly fanning their tail outwards as they walk with incredibly delicate steps.

Avicultural Notes

Recommended aviary size	200 square feet (18.6sq.m)
Number in captivity	876
Full adult plumage	First year
Egg clutch size	6 – 11 eggs
Incubation period	27 – 28 days
Feeding habits	Normal pheasant diet

Mikado Pheasant – *Syrmaticus mikado* (Ogilvie-Grant) 1906 (E)

The Mikado Pheasant whilst less colourful than most other species is nevertheless a most attractive bird with the cocks being predominantly a metallic blue-black colour with bars of white across the wing coverts, rump and tail, and prominent red wattles around the eye. They come only from the island of Taiwan where they live in the mountains at around 6,000 – 10,000 feet (1,800 – 3,000m).

While primarily a bird of the thick forest they seem able to adapt well to secondary bamboo growth and although listed as an endangered species would appear at present to be keeping their numbers fairly steady. As with all the *Syrmaticus* group, they are a hardy and fairly easy aviary bird. Their eggs are remarkable in that although Mikado's are no larger than the other pheasants in the genus their eggs are almost double in size. This species was first recorded in 1906 and first reared in 1913. Early observations indicated that they required considerable amounts of green food but I have never really found this to be the case. They became very scarce between the wars, but a small fresh importation in the 1950s led to a major revival in their numbers in captivity.

Avicultural Notes

Recommended aviary size	200 square feet (18.6sq.m)
Number in captivity	1,170
Full adult plumage	First year
Egg clutch size	5 – 10 eggs
Incubation period	27 days
Feeding habits	Normal pheasant diet

The Copper Pheasant – *Syrmaticus soemmerringi* (Temminck) 1830

In Japan, their country of origin, some 700,000 Copper Pheasants are shot each year. They are bred in pheasant farms in quite large numbers. However, the Japanese like aviculturists all over the world have found them to be a difficult species due to the pugnacious habits

A Scintillating Copper Pheasant seen at Daws Hall.

The Copper Pheasant is attractive but pugnacious to its mate.

of the males. Their solution to the problem has been to keep each bird separate and to breed by artificial insemination.

In spite of their numbers in Japan the Copper Pheasant has proved to be the least prolific of the genus in captivity. There are five sub-species of which the best known are the Scintillating *Syrmaticus soemmerringi scintillans*, the Ijima *Syrmaticus soemmerringi ijimae* and the Soemmerring's *Syrmaticus soemmerringi soemmerringi.* They are a handsome bird and the sun shining on a cock Scintillating Copper Pheasant when he is puffed up during the breeding season is spectacular.

Avicultural Notes

Recommended aviary size	200 square feet (18.6sq.m)
Number in captivity	630 of all sub-species
Full adult plumage	First year
Egg clutch size	6 – 12 eggs
Incubation period	25 days
Feeding habits	Normal pheasant diet

Reeves Pheasant – *Syrmaticus reevesi* (J. E. Gray) 1829

The magnificent Reeves Pheasant is one of the most popular and common of all the pheasants in captivity and is certainly the most numerous of the genus. The tail of the cock bird can grow to a length of five feet and in order to preserve it aviaries should be spacious and, if possible, free from corners. The bird is illustrated on page 3.

They can be pugnacious, although my experience is that in the adult bird this is more likely to be towards humans than its mate; as chicks however they can be very belligerent and should not be associated with chicks of other species.

The Reeves Pheasant comes from central northern China where it lives in the forested mountains from 1,000 – 6,000 feet (300 – 1,800m). There are records of it being kept in captivity as early as 1808. They have been released in pheasant coverts in England and elsewhere and have survived well. They can still be found in areas such as Woburn Park fending for themselves very successfully.

Avicultural Notes

Recommended aviary size	200+ square feet (over 19sq.m)
Number in captivity	2,200
Full adult plumage	First year
Egg clutch size	7 – 14 eggs
Incubation period	25 days
Feeding habits	Normal pheasant diet

THE TRUE PHEASANTS Genus - *Phasianus*

There are two principal species of True Pheasant, *P.colchicus* Linnaeus 1758 and *P.versicolor* Vieillot 1825, and many sub-species, particularly of *P.colchicus*. They are known as a game bird rather than an aviary bird so that a description is unnecessary. It is however worth making two points: the first that they are almost as beautiful as any of the pheasant species; the second that due to man's interference many of the pure sub-species are pure no longer. An example of this is the Formosan Ringneck Pheasant which has now crossed with Chinese Ringneck Pheasants released on the island.

THE RUFFED PHEASANTS Genus - *Chrysolophus*

The Golden Pheasant - *Chrysolophus pictus* (Linnaeus) 1758

The choice of a Golden Pheasant for the cover of this book reflects the popularity of this species as an aviary bird. At the last census carried out by the World Pheasant Association in 1976 there were over 2,000 more Golden Pheasants in captivity than any other ornamental pheasant species. Coming from central China the Golden has long

The Yellow Golden Pheasant Cock is a great aviary favourite.

been kept in aviaries by the Chinese who prized them for their beauty. Flydressers of trout and salmon flies value their feathers for fly tying and ladies their feathers for hat decoration.

As an aviary bird they have a great advantage in appearing to be content and to do well in aviaries of quite small size as well as being totally hardy. Altogether a wonderful and beautiful little pheasant.

A number of mutations have occurred of the Golden Pheasant, such as the Dark Throated, the Salmon and the Yellow Golden. The latter, which was produced by the Italian, Professor Ghigi, is probably the best known and is certainly the most striking.

Avicultural Notes

Recommended aviary size	100 square feet (9.3sq.m)
Number in captivity	6,400
Full adult plumage	Second year
Egg clutch size	6 – 12 eggs
Incubation period	22 days
Feeding habits	Normal pheasant diet

Lady Amherst's Pheasant – *Chrysolophus amherstiae* (Leadbeater) 1829

The Lady Amherst's Pheasant is the nearest competitor, other than the Indian Peafowl, to the Golden Pheasant. Although recorded in 1829, it was not until 1874 that they were first bred. Unfortunately almost all early importations seem to have had more cock birds than hens and many hybrids with golden were produced. As a result of this and probably further hybridisation due to carelessness, there are not as many pure Lady Amherst's Pheasants in captivity as might be wished.

Aviculturally they are very similar to the Golden Pheasant and are just as hardy. In the wild they come from further south in China than the Golden, but tend to live at higher altitudes in bamboo thickets.

Aviculture Notes

Recommended aviary size	100+ square feet (over 9.3sq.m)
Number in captivity	3,177
Full adult plumage	Second year
Egg clutch size	6 – 12 eggs
Incubation period	22 days
Feeding habits	Standard pheasant diet

THE PEACOCK-PHEASANTS Genus - *Polyplectron*

The Bronze-tailed Peacock-Pheasants – *Polyplectron chalcurum* (Lesson) 1831

The Bronze-tailed Peacock-Pheasants are probably the least well known of all the Peacock-Pheasants in aviaries. There are two subspecies, one of which comes from North Sumatra and the other from South Sumatra. Although rather drab brownish-coloured little pheasants, they are, as can be seen in the photograph below very charming birds. They are extremely quiet pheasants to keep, but sadly rare in collections. Indeed at the time of writing I am the proud owner of the only pair in England. However, Mr Charles Sivelle in America has imported several pairs in recent years which are now breeding well.

As with all the Peacock-Pheasants, they produce only two eggs to a clutch but will produce a number of clutches in a year.

Avicultural Notes

Recommended aviary size	100 +square feet (over 9.3sq.m)
Number in captivity	30
Full adult plumage	First year
Egg clutch size	2 eggs
Incubation period	22 days
Feeding habits	Normal pheasant diet plus peanuts, chopped fruit, seeds, mealworms, etc.
Special note	Heat necessary in winter

The Bronze-tailed Peacock-Pheasant is an aviary rarity.

Rothschild's Peacock-Pheasant – *Polyplectron inopinatum* (Rothschild) 1903

From the mountains of the Malay Peninsula where it was said to be far from rare, this pheasant lives in the rugged mountain country. Few have ever been in captivity and little is known about them.

Avicultural Notes

Recommended aviary size	100 – 150 square feet (9.3 – 14sq.m)
Number in captivity	1
Full adult plumage	First year, but less bright
Egg clutch size	Probably 2 eggs
Incubation period	Unknown
Feeding habits	Probably as for other Peacock-Pheasants

Germain's Peacock-Pheasant – *Polyplectron germaini* (Elliot) 1866

The Germain's is slightly similar to the Grey Peacock-Pheasant, but is considerably more drab in colouring and has no crest or ruff. In behaviour they appear to be rather wilder than most of the other Peacock-Pheasants, when kept in captivity, with a habit of flying up and uttering a loud, raucous alarm call if disturbed suddenly. As with all the Peacock-Pheasants a nesting basket several feet off the ground is likely to be preferred to nest boxes on the ground.

They come from eastern Cochin China and southern Annam where they live in forests from sea level to around 4,000 feet (1,200m). Once settled they breed well in captivity. Almost all the captive stock is in America.

Avicultural Notes

Recommended aviary size	100 – 150 square feet (9.3 – 14sq. m)
Number in captivity	190
Full adult plumage	First year
Egg clutch size	2 eggs
Incubation period	22 days
Feeding habits	As for Bronze-tailed Peacock-Pheasants
Special note	A good shelter with possibly some heat advisable in winter

The Grey Peacock-Pheasants – *Polyplectron bicalcaratum* (Linnaeus) 1758

There are five sub-species in this group. The Grey Peacock-Pheasant is often known as the Chinquis and is a really lovely aviary bird. They are by far the most northern in distribution of all the Peacock-Pheasants and are found in damp hill forests and gullies from Sikkim and Burma down to northern Thailand and central Annam.

The very beautiful and much prized Palawan Peacock-Pheasant.

The Chinquis is almost totally hardy although a good dry shelter is advisable. They are delightfully friendly pheasants, constantly displaying regardless of people, and breed freely. As with all the Peacock-Pheasants, clutch sizes are two eggs only, but if eggs are collected as laid, clutches can be obtained about every four weeks for a period. It is better to rear the chicks under a bantam hen. If they are to be incubator and brooder lamp reared some care must be taken in the early stages to hand feed the baby chicks with mealworms or clean maggots.

Avicultural Notes

Recommended aviary size	100 – 150 square feet (9.3 – 14sq. m)
Number in captivity	350
Full adult plumage	First year
Egg clutch size	2 eggs
Incubation period	22 days
Feeding habits	As for Bronze-tailed Peacock-Pheasants

Malay Peacock-Pheasant – *Polyplectron malacense malacense* (Scopoli) 1786

The Malay Peacock-Pheasant is the nominate race of this species and is another fairly rare pheasant in captivity. Over half the present captive population is in America where the Bronx Zoo has been particularly successful in breeding them in humid well-planted aviaries. They are not common in the wild. As their name implies, they come from the Malay Peninsula where they occur from sea level to 3,000 feet (900m), but normally at the lower altitudes in thick forest. The Bornean species *Polyplectron malacense schleiermacheri* is rarer in captivity and is listed as endangered in the wild.

Avicultural Notes

Recommended aviary size	100 – 150 square feet (9.3 – 14sq.m)
Number in captivity	50 of both sub-species
Full adult plumage	First year
Egg clutch size	2 eggs
Incubation period	22 days
Feeding habits	As for other Peacock-Pheasants

Palawan Peacock-Pheasant – *Polyplectron emphanum* (Temminck) 1831 ⚠E

The lovely Palawan Peacock-Pheasant is quite the most colourful and dramatic of all the Peacock-Pheasants. It is found only on the little island of Palawan in the Phillipines, where it inhabits the thick forest at low altitudes.

Forest cutting and destruction combined with trapping is putting the future of this delightful pheasant in jeopardy. Fortunately, numbers in captivity have increased in recent years and several aviculturists have good breeding nuclei. As can be seen from the photograph on page 103 of the cock bird displaying they are a lovely bird to look after and keep.

Avicultural Notes

Recommended aviary size	100 square feet (9.3sq.m)
Numbers in captivity	360
Full adult plumage	Second year
Egg clutch size	2 eggs
Incubation period	18 – 19 days
Feeding habits	As for other Peacock-Pheasants

THE CRESTED ARGUS Genus - *Rheinartia*

Rheinart's Crested Argus – *Rheinartia ocellata ocellata* (Elliot) 1871

The Rheinart's is the nominate race of the two pheasants in this group, the other being the Malay Crested Argus *Rheinartia ocellata nigrescens.* As neither of these pheasants are at present kept in captivity description of them is being omitted.

THE GREAT ARGUS Genus - *Argusianus*

Malay Great Argus – *Argusianus argus argus* (Linneaus) 1766

The display of the cock Great Argus has long been famous. Strangely however when not in display the Malay Great Argus and its close relative, the Bornean Great Argus, are rather unattractive birds. They are large in appearance, in length rather than height, although this is largely brought about by the length of the wing coverts and tail rather than large body size. They weigh little more than a Monal Pheasant but in shape are more like an Indian Blue Peacock.

There are reasonable numbers in captivity although being a large bird and requiring some heat in winter many of those in captivity are in zoological collections. As might be expected from their names, the nominate race comes from the Malay Peninsula and the Bornean Great Argus from the island of Borneo where they live in thick forest from sea level up to 4,000 feet (1,200m). Both species are still fairly common in the wild. There is one other Argus Pheasant, the Double-banded Argus *Argusianus bipunctatus* Wood 1871 but this is only known from a single primary feather at the British Museum.

Avicultural Notes

Recommended aviary size	400 square feet (37sq.m)
Number in captivity	200 of both species
Full adult plumage	Third year
Egg clutch size	2 eggs
Incubation period	24 – 25 days
Feeding habits	As for Firebacks and Peacock-Pheasants

THE PEAFOWL Genus - *Pavo*

Indian or Blue Peafowl – *Pavo cristatus* (Linnaeus) 1758

There is no need to describe the lovely Indian Blue Peafowl which is well known to everyone. Much religious superstition surrounds them and many consider it unlucky to have the tail feathers in the house. In Hindu countries peafowl are considered sacred and are therefore not trapped or hunted. Under these conditions they became very tame. They are easy to keep in aviaries although prone to the disease Blackhead.

Indian Peafowl are really too large to be ideal aviary birds and look their best when at liberty. However they can be damaging to gardens and have the disadvantage of a harsh strident call, particularly in the breeding season. There is one mutation, the Blackwinged, as well as colour variations including the White and the Pied.

Avicultural Notes

Recommended aviary size	400+ square feet (over 37sq.m)
Number in captivity	4,100+
Full adult plumage	Third year
Egg clutch size	4 – 8 eggs
Incubation period	27 – 29 days
Feeding habits	Normal pheasant diet

Green Peafowl – *Pavo muticus* (Linnaeus) 1766 (E)

The Green Peafowl are even more beautiful birds than the Blue. They are, however, a great deal rarer and in parts of their range in the Malay Peninsula are now very scarce. Fortunately their distribution is a large one from Burma in the north to the island of

The truly spectacular Javanese Green Peafowl (*Pavo muticus muticus*).

Java in the south. Like their cousins, the Blue Peafowl, they live at lowish altitudes rarely ascending above 3,000 – 4,000 feet (900 – 1,200m).

There are three sub-species, the Javanese *Pavo muticus muticus* and Indo-Chinese *Pavo muticus imperator*, which are fairly similar, and the Burmese *Pavo muticus spicifer* which is more drab in colouring. Although they are rarer in captivity than the Indian Blue they are nevertheless well represented, particularly in zoological collections.

Avicultural Notes

Recommended aviary size	400 square feet (37sq.m)
Number in captivity	500 (all sub-species)
Full adult plumage	Third year
Egg clutch size	4 – 6 eggs
Incubation period	28 days
Feeding habits	As for Peacock-Pheasants
Special note	Not as hardy as the Indian or Blue Peafowl and some heat in winter and a good shelter is to be recommended.

THE CONGO PEAFOWL Genus - *Afropavo*

Congo Peacock – *Afropavo congensis* (Chapin) 1936

The Congo Peacock is the only one of the forty-eight species of pheasant which does not come from Asia but comes as its name implies from the Congo basin. From 1913 until 1936 it was only known of from one feather and even this had not been identified. It was Dr James P. Chapin who found the feather, found a stuffed pair wrongly named in the Congo Museum, and finally positively identified the species.

They are very different from the Green or Blue Peafowl, having in the case of the male a bristly crest and no long train of tail feathers. Both cock and hen are chunky birds with their beauty lying in their colouring rather than their shape.

The principal captive nucleus is in Antwerp Zoo and there is little likelihood of the average pheasant aviculturist ever obtaining them.

Avicultural Notes

Recommended aviary size	200 square feet (18.6sq.m)
Number in captivity	35
Full adult plumage	Second year
Egg clutch size	3 – 4 eggs
Incubation period	26 days
Feeding habits	As for the Peacock-Pheasants
Special note	Success with this species seems to lie with having spacious heated inside accommodation with humidity control

E·H·

Appendix 1

THE WORLD PHEASANT ASSOCIATION

Those readers who may wish to join an Association concerned with the future survival of the pheasant species as well as their avicultural care could do no better than join the World Pheasant Association. With membership in over forty countries, and branches in many parts of the U.K. as well as in Europe, this lively Association provides the opportunity for interested people to meet and exchange views.

Aims of the World Pheasant Association

To develop, promote and support conservation of all species of the Order *Galliformes* with initial emphasis on the Family *Phasianidae* by:

1. Encouraging sound and improved methods of aviculture both in the countries of origin and elsewhere.
2. Establishing a data-bank for the *Galliformes* and acting as an advisory body to members of the Association and to outside organisations on all matters relating to the ecology, conservation, protection and breeding of these birds.
3. Promoting constructive research in the wild and through aviculture, and publishing the results in the interests of conservation.
4. Educating the public by all means to a better appreciation of *Galliformes* in particular and nature in general.
5. Establishing reserve collections and buffer stocks of threatened or endangered species under the surveillance of the Association and in collaboration with the governments of the countries of origin and approved breeders.

The Priorities will be determined by the Council of WPA in consultation with governments concerned and in close collaboration with international bodies such as ICBP (International Council for Bird Preservation), IUCN (International Union for Conservation of Nature and Natural Resources) and WWF (World Wildlife Fund).

Membership of the WPA

This is open to all those in sympathy with the objects of the Association and willing to comply with its rules. WPA is an international co-operative organisation designed to enable all interested persons and institutions to participate in fulfilling the objectives of the Association. WPA is fast becoming accepted as the most effective organisation for Pheasant conservation in the World.

Advantages of Membership of WPA

These include:

(a) Access to a data-bank of information on pheasants and related birds.
(b) Expert advice on all matters pertaining to aviculture of pheasants and related birds.
(c) Attending an annual conference in Great Britain or elsewhere.
(d) The opportunity to visit pheasant collections and conservation areas throughout the world.
(e) An annual journal and two newsletters a year.
(f) The opportunity to participate in special conservation programmes at home and overseas as determined by Council and Governments concerned.
(g) Attendance at the AGM and participation in the election of officers in accordance with the Rules of the Association.
(h) Other privileges as decided by the Council from time to time.

For Subscription rates and further information please write to:

The Secretary
The World Pheasant Association
Daws Hall
Lamarsh
Nr. Bures
Suffolk C08 5EX

BIBLIOGRAPHY

Austin Jnr O. L.
Birds of the World. Hamlyn Pub. Co., London and New York

Delacour J.
Pheasants: Their Care and Breeding. T. F. H. Pub. Inc., Neptune, New Jersey, U.S.A.
The Pheasants of the World. Spur Pub. Co., Liss, Hampshire

Gerrits H. A.
Pheasants including their Care in the Aviary. Blandford Press, Poole, Dorset

Rodriguez de la Fuente F.
Animals of the Jungle. Orbis Pub. Co., London

Stromberg J.
A Guide to Better Hatching. Stromberg Pub. Co., Fort Dodge, Iowa, U.S.A.

Stromberg L.
Sexing Birds. Stromberg Pub. Co., Fort Dodge, Iowa, U.S.A.

Trevisick C. H.
Fancy Pheasants, Jungle Fowl and Peafowl for Beginners. Cage & Aviary Birds/Poultry World, London

Wayre P.
A Guide to the Pheasants of the World. Country Life Pub., London

Wright L.
The Illustrated Book of Poultry. Cassell, Petter and Galpin, London and New York

INDEX OF SCIENTIFIC NAMES

INDEX OF COMMON NAMES

GENERAL INDEX

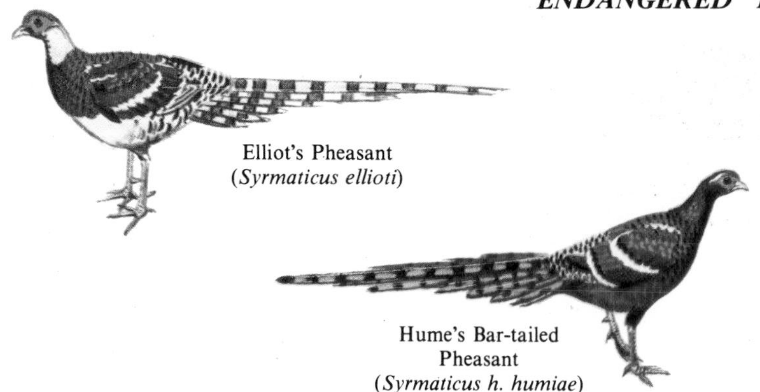

Elliot's Pheasant
(*Syrmaticus ellioti*)

Hume's Bar-tailed
Pheasant
(*Syrmaticus h. humiae*)

Brown Eared-Pheasant
(*Crossoptilon mantchuricum*)

Swinhoe's Pheasant
(*Lophura swinhoei*)

Edwards' Pheasant
(*Lophura edwardsi*)

Chinese Monal
(*Lophophorus lhuysi*)

Sclater's Monal
(*Lophophorus sclateri*)

Western Tragopan
(*Tragopan melancephalus*)

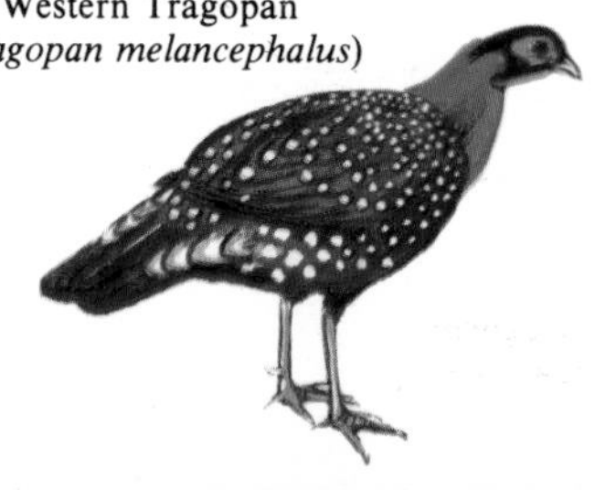